VINTAGE MERLO

VINTAGE MERLO

Reflections on a life well-lived

HARRY A. MERLO
with Kerry Tymchuk

HARRY A. MERLO FOUNDATION
Portland, Oregon

Co-writer: Kerry Tymchuk
Cover image: Lorenzo E. Ghiglieri
Cover design: Machele Brass, Brass Design
Text design: Anita Jones, Another Jones Graphics

Library of Congress Number:

ISBN: 1-00-430012-9

Printed and bound in the United States
by Bridgetown Printing

Harry A. Merlo Foundation
1001 SE Sandy Boulevard
Portland, Oregon 97214
(503) 963-9463

This statue of Mama graces the Clotilde Merlo Park in Stirling City, California.

TO MAMA, WHO MADE IT ALL POSSIBLE.

CONTENTS

FOREWORD

My name is Cori Alexander, and I am a recent graduate of the University of Portland in Portland, Oregon, and a proud member of the 2005 NCAA National Championship women's soccer team. I am honored that Harry Merlo, who is friends with many famous and influential business and political leaders, has asked me to write the foreword to his autobiography.

I am just one of many people who can say that "Harry Merlo made a positive difference in my life." The fact is that college would merely have been a dream for me had I not received the Harry Merlo Women's Soccer Scholarship.   A while back, I wrote Mr. Merlo a thank you note, just to be sure he truly knew how much his generosity meant. I was surprised when I received a letter from him in return. He thanked me for my note, and he shared a story about his mother, who would save her pennies and nickels and dimes in a jar, and twice a year would donate that money to Boys Town in Omaha, Nebraska. She told her children, "If you won't share a dollar, you'll never share a million."

Those words inspired me then, and they inspire me still. In fact, they inspired me to give a speech at the University of Portland where I pledged to Mr. Merlo that I would pay his generosity back by walking in his footsteps, by making a difference in the lives of others, and by challenging my peers to do the same. I told my "twenty something" friends and teammates that we may not have much money, but we can still be a positive force. We can help out at a local Ronald McDonald House, volunteer at the Humane Society, or kick the soccer ball around with a child in need of a role model.

I believe the reason Mr. Merlo asked me to write this foreword is to issue the same challenge to all those who read this book. I am honored to do just that. If you enjoy "Vintage Merlo" as much as I did...if you find inspiration in the courage and common sense of Mama Merlo and in the remarkable life story of her son, Harry, then I challenge you to "pay it forward" and to give of your time, talents and treasure.

The Archbishop Desmond Tutu once said, "Do your little bit of good where you are; it's those little bits of good put together that overwhelm the world." I invite you to join with Mr. Merlo and me in overwhelming the world!

PROLOGUE

I was born and raised in a lumber yard.

NO MATTER HOW MANY times I shared that claim with friends, colleagues and business associates during the course of my half-century career in the forest products industry, I always knew that quite a few assumed their leg was being pulled. And while I confess to having spun a tall tale or two about my humble origins, there is no denying that from the day of my birth in March 1925 until the day I joined the United States Marine Corps some eighteen years later, my life was spent in the shadow of the Diamond Match Lumber Company in Stirling City, California.

Looking back on it, I suppose there are two reactions someone could have to growing up in a lumberyard. One would be to get as far away as possible from an industry that long had a reputation as one of the most dangerous and backbreaking of occupations. The other would be to do what I did--embrace a challenging industry and take pride in the important role it has played in the American story.

I have been richly blessed in my life with a remarkable and courageous mother; a sister and four brothers, each with a special place in my heart; a wonderful son and daughter-in-law; two grandchildren who I delight in spoiling; lifelong friends; the opportunity to travel the world; and professional and financial success beyond what I could ever have imagined. Yes, I have also suffered a few setbacks, but

I regard these as part of a full life. All in all, I know how fortunate I am and what a grand adventure I have had.

While I realize there are far fewer tomorrows than yesterdays in my life, I also am not ready to sit quietly by the fireplace with a shawl around my shoulders. Henry Ford once said, "Anyone who stops learning is old, whether at twenty or eighty. Anyone who keeps learning is young. The greatest thing in life is to keep your mind young." From walking through the vineyards of my winery, to logging, landscaping and planting new seedlings on my ranches, to making new business investments, to searching for causes worthy of the philanthropic support of the Merlo Foundation, not a day passes by when I am not learning something or trying to reach a new goal. In fact, I have concluded that life, like a good wine, just keeps getting better with age.

One of the goals I set for myself some time ago, was to write my life story and share it with family and friends. I wanted to do this not to call any attention to any accomplishments I might have achieved in my life and career. Rather, I share my story because it allows me to pay tribute to individuals like my mother who guided me on my journey, and to salute a country that makes even the biggest dreams come true.

I invite you to pull up a comfortable chair, pour yourself a glass of wine—a nice Lago di Merlo Merlot would be fitting—and join me on my journey.

My parents, Joe and Clotilde Merlo

CHAPTER 1

From Italy to America

My parents were born twelve years and twelve miles apart from each other. My father, Giuseppe Angelo Merlo, entered the world on December 12, 1881, in Capriata d'Orba, Italy, a picturesque village built on the ruins of an ancient Roman town on the River Orba. My mother, Giuseppa Amalia Clotilde Camussa, was born on July 19, 1893 in the village of Bosco Marengo.

My father was the oldest of six children, ahead of Giovanni, Emilio, Pietro, Angelina, and Albina. His parents—my grandparents—struggled to make a living off their land by cultivating grapes, wheat and corn, and by raising cattle. Hard work led to modest success, and when my father was ten, the Merlo family entered the timber business for the first time, as my grandfather bought a parcel of land that was home to stands of oak trees. In addition to selling fine bolts of solid oak, the family stripped small poles from large limbs and sold them to farmers as stakes to support grapes and other crops.

The Catholic Church was at the center of village life, and local parish priests provided educational instruction to children throughout the year. It was understood, however, that farm work was to come before schoolwork, and most studying was done by candlelight at night, after the day's labor in the field was complete. My father was an eager student, and especially enjoyed the works of Dante, which he absorbed to the point that he could recite extensive verses of "The Divine Comedy" well into his eighties.

My father's passion for literature was matched by his passion for music. As he grew up, he developed a fine tenor voice, and sang in a traditional strolling music group that performed in nearby villages. His plans to seek a musical career by taking voice lessons in Milan were put on hold in 1901 when he began the service commitment to the Italian military that was required of all young men in Italy. He joined the Guardia de Finansa—the Italian revenue service—and spent many a dangerous night apprehending smugglers on the Swiss border.

While my father was in the Guardia, his brother, Emilio, joined the influx of Europeans seeking a new life in America. Emilio made his way west from New York's Ellis Island to San Francisco, where other recent immigrants from Italy told him about work opening up at the Diamond Match Lumber Company plant in Chico, California and at their huge new sawmill under construction in Stirling City, California. Emilio found employment there, and wrote to his brother of the wonders and freedom of America. When my father was discharged from the Guardia in 1906, he decided to abandon his plans for music and voice training, and to join Emilio in America.

The eighteen-day crossing of the Atlantic was a rough one for "Citta di Napoli," (City of Naples) the ship that would bring my father to America. Four women passengers died of shock when the vessel took in water and listed to one side for four hours. The heavy seas and harrowing moments were made tolerable for my father by the fact that another passenger on the ship was famed opera singer Enrico Caruso. One of the most celebrated figures of his time, Caruso was en route to a concert tour in America. My father would later recall that when the evening seas were calm, Caruso would often delight his fellow passengers with an impromptu performance.

Upon arrival at Ellis Island, my father changed his first name to its English equivalent, "Joseph," and he would be known as "Joe" for the rest of his life. He traveled via train to Sacramento, and then to Chico, where he and his brother were joyously reunited.

My dad arrived in America speaking no English, and his first purchase in California was a book to teach him his new language. With his brother's help, he found work as a laborer with Diamond Match Lumber Company, building storage sheds and helping in the millwork department.

He worked hard during the day and dreamed of gold during the night. When he was eight years old, my father spied a man panning for gold in the creek near his home, and it sparked a lifelong fascination with the precious metal. Perhaps it was pre-ordained that after two years of working hard and saving his money, my father, entranced by stories of fortunes being made in gold mining, moved eighty miles south to the small California community of Forest Hill so he could seek the "mother lode."

Four years after arriving in the heart of gold country, my then 33-year-old father met and married 22-year-old Cissy Halstead, the daughter of a Norweigan immigrant father and a California native mother. Most of their married life was to be spent battling tough economic conditions, with an occasional month or two of prosperity whenever the mine revealed a vein of gold. The marriage was blessed with a son, Amiel, and a daughter, Caroline. Amiel was all of seven years old and Caroline just five, when their mother died in 1921 after suffering a traumatic miscarriage.

Tragedy was also to strike the life of my mother, who also spent her early years in Italy helping her family make a living off the land. At a very young age, she learned the skills of grape harvesting for wine making, cultivating crops, tending animals and cooking for the family. Called "Tilde" by all her friends, my mother was full of fun and reputed to be one of the finest dancers at the local community hall. It was at the hall where fate intervened and she met and fell in love with Pietro Merlo, my father's youngest brother. They were married in 1914 as storm clouds gathered over Europe. In 1915, one month before the birth of their son, Pierino, Italy declared war on Austria-Hungary and Pietro Merlo joined countless thousands of other Italian young men in marching off to war. Pietro's unit was sent to the front lines on the Austrian border. As the war dragged on month after month, Pietro would send many letters to his wife, expressing his love, and inquiring about the health of his son—a son he would never live to see as Pietro was killed in combat in January of 1918.

Devastated by the loss of her husband, my mother returned to her childhood home, where she and her son lived with her mother, supplementing her small military widow's pension with work as a domestic. There she remained for three years, honing the culinary skills she learned as a child. She lived a life of carefully defined social boundaries in villages where the mayor, the priest and the schoolmaster were held above all others. If she and her son were to pass any of these officials on the street, young Pierino would be expected to stop, remove his cap and bow to the dignitaries out of respect and tradition. Tilde began to save her money in hopes of one day being able to seek a new life in America, where Pierino would have the opportunity to grow up having to bow to no one.

Following the death of his wife, my father continued to work in the gold mine so he could put food on the table for his children. He understood, however, that the children needed a mother every bit as much as they needed food, and his thoughts turned to his brother's widow. He had loved and respected Pietro, and though he had never met Tilde, he knew instinctively that any woman his brother married must be very special. He eventually mustered up the nerve to write to Tilde and to propose marriage, promising that a better life awaited her in America.

Tilde accepted the offer, and she and her son landed at Ellis Island on October 14, 1921, where Pierino took the name "Pete." A seven-day train trip across their new country was to take them to Sacramento. Traveling across the Atlantic by ship and then across America by train was not an exact science, and all that my father knew was what Tilde had written him—that she had accepted his proposal, that she and her son would soon be departing from Italy, and that when they arrived in New York, they would then make their way via train to Sacramento. To be assured that he would not miss their arrival, my father took a job at the railroad station, and for week after week he would meet every train that pulled into station, hoping it was carrying his bride-to-be. At last, the passengers he was looking for arrived on October 21, 1921, and my mother met my father for the first time. The two families became one in a civil ceremony the very next day.

⁂

Here I am at age 3, already dreaming of a career in the timber industry.

CHAPTER 2

Born in a Lumberyard

THE FIRST YEAR OF MARRIAGE was a very difficult one for the new Merlo family. My father continued to labor in a series of mines, but the work was irregular and the pay was meager. Pete would later recall, "In Italy we had polenta three times a day—once as hot mush with milk, once sliced cold like cornbread, and once fried with whatever else we could get. When we came to California, I went to bed hungry and cried myself to sleep every night. I came to America with wooden shoes, and when they wore out, my shoes were barley sacks and newspapers that Joe Merlo wrapped around my feet. I kept telling Mother we had to go back to Italy." Into that grinding poverty my older brother, John, was born on August 1, 1922—nine months and one week after our parents were married.

The financial situation of the blended Merlo family, which now included four children—Amiel, age 7; Pete, age 6; Caroline, age 5; and newborn John-- was only to get worse. Money was so tight that my mother could not make bread because she could not afford to buy flour. Pete and Amiel would later recall that they would go to nearby fruit orchards and pick apples and pears, which my mother would serve as the main course at dinner. Despite Pete's efforts to help, my father developed an intense and unreasonable jealousy of him, at times even forbidding him to eat whatever meager supper was being served.

On more than one occasion, my mother was forced to smuggle food to Pete after my father had gone to bed.

The only thing that had changed in the Merlo family situation two years later was that another baby was on the way. In desperation, my mother turned for help to my father's brother, Emilio, who still had a good job at the mill in Stirling City, California, but who had fallen sick and needed someone to care for him, since he had left his wife and three children in Italy until he could save enough money to pay their passage to America. My mother offered to help out, if she and my father could move their family into Emilio's house. Emilio agreed, and the penniless Merlo family abandoned their home to the county for taxes owed, and moved to Stirling City, where Emilio also arranged for my father to get a job on the "green chain" at the mill. For ten hours a day, six days a week, my father would wrestle fresh-cut heavy boards into bins. It was tough, backbreaking work, but it came with a steady paycheck, and by the time I was born on March 5, 1925, there was money enough to provide food for the Merlo family table. A good thing, too, as I weighed in at an impressive fourteen pounds at birth, and had a healthy appetite from the start. My mother would often joke that when I was born, I was already big enough to pile lumber—and there was no doubt that lumber was what Stirling City was all about.

Built by Diamond Match Company in 1901 as a combination logging and milling center, Stirling City was perched some 3,575 feet above sea level on the slopes of the western Sierra Nevadas. Construction of the gigantic sawmill occurred simultaneously with the building of a thirty two mile railroad track which would connect Stirling City with the larger community of Chico via the Butte County Railroad—a necessary link to haul the mill's fresh-cut lumber output down to the

Sacramento Valley for remanufacturing into finished lumber. As the company's name suggested, much of the lumber was used to produce matches, for which there seemed to be an insatiable demand.

Named by a Diamond Match official, who was impressed with a boiler used at one of their Ohio operations made by the Stirling Boiler Company, Stirling City was a "company town" in almost every sense of the word. Diamond Match installed the water and sewer systems, graded streets to prevent deep ruts, and donated materials for construction of the firehouse, train depot, dance pavilion, school, post office, and jail. The grocery and mercantile store and the community bank were owned by the company, as were most of the homes, which were then leased to company employees. Hoping to keep order among the notoriously rough-and-tumble timber workers, company officials made certain through lease covenants that only one business in town—a saloon called "The Red Devil"—could sell liquor on its premises.

The town grid was pear-shaped, seven blocks long and five blocks wide at the north end, three blocks wide in the middle, and two blocks wide at the south end. North-south streets were fittingly named after trees: Spruce, Pine, Oak, Manzanita, Laurel and Fir; east-west streets were named after minerals: Gypsum, Mica, Slate, Lava, Granite, Quartz, and Diamond.

No matter what road you were on, however, your attention was directed at one spot—the Diamond Match sawmill. It took four hundred employees to operate the facility, which included a series of huge steam boilers powering a 1,200 horsepower engine which drove a 22 foot flywheel with a main belt four feet wide and nearly a mile of smaller leather links which turned machinery throughout the mill. The mill pond covered 15 acres, nearly full to the brim with huge logs floating half-submerged.

✯ ✯ ✯ ✯

Company executives and managers lived up town in the tidy homes that comprised Stirling City proper. My uncle's home, where I was born, and the small home a few hundred feet east of his, where my family moved four months after my birth, were literally and figuratively on the "wrong side of the tracks," bordered on the north and east by rail spurs and stack upon stack of some 16 million board feet of drying lumber.

You could walk out our front door straight into the unfenced mill yard where the closest lumber stacks stood not fifty feet from our porch steps. Out our back door was a boardwalk that connected us to the twenty or so other homes—all owned and rented out by the company—that made up our neighborhood. The last names of the families renting those houses were Negretti, Lombardi, Tosello, Sartori, Gallina, Gobato, Cavali, and Simonetti. Collectively, the group of homes was known as "Dago Town."

"Dago" was a slur that was commonly applied to Italian-Americans and its frequent usage in the early 20th century reflected widespread nationwide prejudice. In Stirling City, and elsewhere, Italian immigrants were relegated to the hardest and most menial of jobs—stacking lumber and loading railcars. As segregated minorities tend to do, the Italian immigrants of Stirling City formed close bonds, becoming one large family, giving each other aid and comfort, and, despite the discrimination we often faced, developing a fierce patriotism for their new country.

My siblings and I were to witness and experience a great deal of prejudice during our childhood years, and I learned a few lessons on compassion and leadership from the rare company official who treated my family and other Italian immigrants with dignity and fairness. Though it was over 75 years ago when I saw Dick Colgan, one of the mill managers, treat my mother with great dignity, I can still remember it like yesterday. He didn't call Mama a "dago" like many others did. He called her "Mrs. Merlo." Examples such as this led me to vow at an early age that if ever given the opportunity to be a boss, I would honor and respect the dignity of each worker.

✶✶✶✶

CHAPTER 3

Mama

ABRAHAM LINCOLN ONCE observed, "Everything I am I owe to my mother." I know exactly what he meant. Honesty. Integrity. Hard work. Personal responsibility. Love of God. Love of family. These are the values I have tried to uphold throughout my life. They are values that were instilled in my siblings and me each and every day of our childhood by our mother—or "Mama" as we were to always call her.

My father was forty-three when I was born, and had lived through some exceedingly hard times. Years of physically demanding jobs in the mills and in the mines had taken much out of him, and the lumberyard foreman eventually assigned him easier tasks. Still, he would often complain of poor health, and some of my earliest memories include my father staying home all day due to severe stomach pains. Fewer days at work invariably translated to smaller paychecks, and with five mouths to feed, my mother soon realized she would have to pick up the slack in order to make ends meet.

Although our house was small, Mama decided to take in a boarder, and once word spread about the quality of her cooking, more were soon knocking on the door. When the house next door to ours became available, Mama rented that, too, and filled it with boarders. It wasn't long before she was cooking for her husband, five children, and eight to ten boarders. The vast majority of these were immigrants from Scandanavia or Germany, many of them who only spoke their native language. Somehow, through a mixture of Italian, Norweigan, Swedish, German, and English, Mama was able to communicate with the boarders, and a number of them became almost like family to us.

I have yet to meet anyone who worked as hard as Mama. She would begin each day by kindling the fires in the wood-burning range and fixing breakfast for her family and boarders. (While two Westinghouse steam-operator generators at the sawmill provided electricity for the mill and the "better neighborhoods" of Stirling City, electricity would not come to Dago Town until I was nearly out of high school.) Once the boarders were off to work, she swept the kitchen and living room floors in preparation for the daily mopping, while Amiel made beds, Pete did the laundry—which included scrubbing clothes on the washboard and hanging them outside to dry—and Caroline helped clean the dishes. There was no sink, only two big round washtubs—one for washing, and one for rinsing. When the morning chores were done, Amiel, Pete and Caroline would leave for school, and John and I would remain at home, helping as best we could. I vividly recall going down to the cellar to bring up fruit and jarred goods to the kitchen and gathering vegetables with Mama in our garden. And there are times when I think I can still smell what was located next to our garden--the rabbit hutches, goat corral, and the chicken coop that held up to 1,000 chickens.

The garden and the animals were a matter of life and death, as when the snowdrifts would invariably pile up each November or December, logging would stop in the high Sierras. And without logs, the mill would shut down until the first of March. With no work, the only cash available for three or four months was what had been carefully saved from my father's wages and the room-and-board income. Throughout the long winter, we would depend upon the vegetables that Mama had canned during the summer and fall, or the pears and apples that were stored under blankets of straw, with the snow acting as a natural refrigerator.

Staples, like flour and sugar, were purchased from the community mercantile. Amiel, as the oldest, had the responsibility of walking to the store to pick up the groceries. Mama would give him the list of things she needed, and tell him exactly how much money he needed to retrieve from the coffee cans in which she stored her coins. She was very good with numbers, and always seemed to know precisely what everything would cost.

What Mama didn't get from the mercantile, she would buy from a peddler who would drive into Stirling City every so often with his wares precariously loaded on his truck. Although our home was at the beginning of his Stirling City route, Mama told him to call upon her only when he was heading out of town. Mama—who always advised us to "waste nothing" would then buy the meats that nobody else wanted—soup bones, tripe, and liver. She had also concluded that he would be more willing to cut a deal and lower his prices as he left town, as she knew that the peddler's next stop was Chico, over 36 miles down a very windy mountain road, and he would be motivated to reduce some of the weight of his load. I would later reflect that with her business mind, Mama would have made a great CEO of Louisiana-Pacific.

As I reached four and five years of age, Mama would let me wander on my own, and I would spend most of my day exploring the lumber yard. It was a place of magical sights and unforgettable sounds, and I couldn't wait until I was old enough to work alongside the big strong men who expertly piled giant stacks of lumber to the sky. I loved to walk down to the railroad track to watch the train go by—and I loved it even more when the conductor would occasionally throw me a piece of candy.

I've been accused of having an independent streak, and I guess it was evident early on from an incident that occurred when I was four or five years old. I wanted to walk uptown to get the mail at the Post Office, but Mama wouldn't let me do it. To get back at her, I hid under the boardwalk in a little ditch where I knew Mama couldn't find me, and soon fell asleep. Mama eventually became alarmed when I didn't return home. From our house it was just a few hundred yards to the edge of the canyon down into the west branch of the Feather River, and people had been known to just disappear around there and never be seen again. Mama had them blow the emergency whistle at the mill and mill employees stopped work to join the search for me. I finally woke up when I heard one of the searchers hollering my name. Mama was greatly relieved to see me—but not so relieved that she also didn't give me a swat on the rear.

The constant clatter of rail cars, the slapping of boards upon board, the whine of the bandsaw, and the rhythmic bang of steam-driven machinery: these are sounds that I can still hear when I close my eyes and think of my early childhood. I can also hear my father's yelling. My father had a temper that often got the best of him. Even from an early age, I could sense the tension in our house. My brothers and sister and I never knew what would set our father off, so we were always on our best behavior when he was home. Physical punishment was quick to follow any misbehavior. My brothers and I would sometimes break the low hanging limbs of trees near our house, thereby denying my father the "switches" he would use to inflict punishment. Mama assured us all that our father loved us, even though he rarely, if ever, showed us or her any affection. "That's just your father's way," she would say.

I suppose part of the reason for the constant chip on my father's shoulder was the fact that he was a proud man, and he was embarrassed that he was forced to struggle to support his family. My father was also from an era and a culture where the first-born son was to inherit everything and expected to be the family leader, but economic circumstances forced him on several occasions to rely on the generosity and charity of his younger brother. The Italian husband was also expected to be the family breadwinner, with his wife's place was very much in the kitchen. Ironically, my father's pride would take another blow when Mama's abilities in the kitchen would eventually lead to her bringing in more money to the family coffers than he did.

My mother was not just a good cook, she was probably the best Italian cook in Northern California at the time. When Mama came to America she brought with her recipes she had learned as a child, and those she had learned while serving as a domestic when she was a young widow. Mama was raised in the Piedmont region of Italy, and the cuisine of that region is a unique blend of the simple and the sophisticated. The boarders who lived in our house could not get enough of Mama's cooking, and they soon began to spread the word that the ravioli with a dough that was stretched thin and stuffed with meat and vegetables was the best they ever tasted. People from as far away as Chico were soon asking if Mama could cater their dinners for them. It wasn't long before Mama decided to turn our home into a restaurant on weekends. The price was a dollar a dinner, which included a bottle of my father's home-made wine. Business was brisk, as people would drive thirty-six miles up a winding mountain road or take the train when snow closed the road just to taste Mama's cooking.

(While I couldn't attach a bottle of wine to this book, you will find several of Mama's favorite recipes included as a final chapter.)

Because we did not have a telephone, customers would instead call the nearby mercantile and make reservations with Mr. Musselman, the grocer. He would then send a messenger down to our home to say, "There's four coming on Saturday at one o'clock, and there will be five coming at three o'clock on Sunday." Mama would then begin to work her magic. She would start cooking a big roast beef in one pot and a big pork roast in another. Throughout the day, she would pour wine and home made tomato sauce over the meat. Finally, you wouldn't be able to see the roast or the pork because the sauce was six inches higher than the meat. Toward the last, she would add fresh wild mushrooms that my brothers and I had picked. She would then strain the sauce through a colander, and the meat would go through a meat grinder, and she would use both to fill ravioli. My brothers and sister and I would help Mama cook, keep things clean, serve the customers, and crank up the Victrola to play 78-rpm Italian opera records. If we ever got lazy, Mama would say to us in Italian—"Va presto!"—which meant "Go Faster!" We heard "Va presto!" a lot. Above the entry to the kitchen was a sign that made very clear Mama's expectations of us: It stated: "Chi non lavora, non deve mangiare." The English translation: "If you don't work, you don't eat."

Hunting and fishing made significant contributions to the dinner table. Mama carried in her head the recipe for a Italian specialty— Trotelle alla Savoia—which was trout based with mushrooms and shallots, and was truly a dish fit for royalty. My brothers and I would regularly make the mile long hike down to the Feather River for some of the best trout fishing in the Sierras. As I grew old enough to handle a hunting rifle I would hunt the deer that were so plentiful in the area, and bring home venison for our dinner table and for Mama's restaurant. We lived by the land—and we respected the land. I recall Mama warning us as my brothers and I would leave to go fishing to always use the outhouse and to never pollute the stream. "God is in the water," she would admonish.

My father could easily have been convinced that God was also in the wine, as he gradually became known as Stirling City's best winemaker—it was less demanding than working in the mill yard, and at a dollar a bottle, it was a highly profitable business, even though it remained illegal bootlegging until 1933, when Prohibition was repealed. I suppose there were many times during our childhood when my brothers and I were accomplices to the crime of bootlegging, as my father would often set a washtub on the floor and fill it with 50 pounds of zinfandel grapes. I would then get in the tub and stomp the grapes with my bare feet, giving Dad's wine a very personal touch!

My father's wine was popular because he was a careful and thorough vintner. He removed sediment by siphoning methods sophisticated for their time, and he let his wine age gracefully in oak barrels we stored in our cellar. Between batches, he cleaned the barrels thoroughly, treating them with an infusion of boiled peach leaves to keep the new wine from turning to vinegar. His winemaking venture was such a success that he eventually rented another small home to serve as a storehouse for his product, and Amiel and Pete would spend nights there for a number of years to prevent local residents from absconding with free samples.

Amiel and Pete would also assist my father in the making of grappa, a traditional byproduct of Italian winemaking. Grappa is distilled from the grape skins, stems and seeds that are the residue of winemaking, and it packs quite a punch. In fact, when Amiel and

Pete emptied the grappa into jars, they had to guard against becoming intoxicated on the mere fumes. I would have my own experience with grappa each year at Christmas time. During the holidays, it was a tradition to walk around Dago Town calling on our neighbors. There was always snow on the ground in December, so my brothers and I would walk in front of Mama and Dad, breaking a trail for them. At each house, Mama and Dad would be offered a small glass of grappa, and the children would get a little cherry that had been preserved in the alcohol. By the time we got to the fifth or sixth house, and had several more cherries, my brothers and I would begin to feel kind of silly, and frequently fall into the snow. We forged a very crooked trail in the snow as we returned to our house after visiting the last neighbor.

⁂

Growing up in "Dago Town"

I STILL REMEMBER MY first day of class in Stirling City's two-room elementary school. (First through third grade students were in one room; fourth through eighth grade in the other.) I had watched my brothers go off to school while I remained at home, and counted the days until I could start first grade. When that day came, I soon discovered there was one big problem: I had grown up speaking Italian as my first language, and my English was still rudimentary at best. There were fifteen students in my first grade class, and the only one who understood me—or who I fully understood—was my friend Willie Vardanega. The last names of my other classmates included Duncan, Scott, Brown, Kenworthy, Hollinger, and Lewis. Needless to say, none of them spoke a word of Italian.

Children can be cruel to outsiders, and these kids were no exception. Willie and I were frequently teased about our inability to speak English, our accents, our Catholicism, and our heritage. It didn't help matters much when our teacher, Miss Collins, in a misguided attempt to make us feel more welcome, asked Willie and me to sing a song in front of the class. We sang in Italian a chorus that we had heard some of our neighbors sing after they had a glass or two of wine. The song sounded something like this: "Geovinezza, giovinezza,

Primavera di bellezza, Della vita nell' asprezza, il tuo canto squilla e va! ("Youth, youth, springtime of beauty, from a life of harshness, your own song shall ring out in victory.") It wasn't until years later when we would learn that this song, which we liked because it had a catchy melody, was actually entitled, "Giovinezza: Triumphal Anthem of the National Fascist Party," and was a favorite song of Italian dictator Benito Mussolini.

Singing aside, I was a very serious student who remembered what my Mama reminded me of on many mornings, "We work hard at work, you work hard at school." Not only did I work hard, but I played hard, too. Staying physically fit was a necessity if I were to hold my own in the fist fights that sometimes were a result of the taunting I received from classmates.

My first years in school were 1931-32, years in which the Great Depression was gripping the United States and the world. Thanks to shrewd decisions made by the managers of Diamond Match, the Stirling City operation was one of the few mills in America that was able to continue to run at capacity. The ongoing operation of the mill meant that people had enough money to continue to buy my father's wine and to patronize Mama's restaurant on the weekend. Indeed, by the time I finished first grade, the Merlo family finances, while still shaky, had never been better. By then, Amiel had been out on his own for a year or so, and Pete, who still lived at home, made good money stacking lumber at the mill. (Pete always provided me with a role model when it came to hard work and persistence. I recall that when he had his first date with Mary Leone—his high school girlfriend and eventual wife—he had no car or means of transportation so he walked the 36 miles from Stirling City to Chico, where Mary Leone lived with her parents. Unfortunately, he arrived late and Mary Leone had already left for the movie, so he had no alternative but to turn around and walk the 36 miles back to Stirling City!)

The problem was that all the money that Mama made at the restaurant and that Pete brought home was under the ultimate control of my father. This was not an individual quirk of his, rather it was an Italian custom left over from the Roman times. There was nothing customary, however, about the lengths to which Dad would go to keep control of any money made by a family member. When Pete announced he wanted to move out, Dad convinced him to stay and to keep giving him the money from his paychecks. If he did, Dad promised Pete that when he got married, he would give Pete and his new wife $1,000, and that he would buy them a new house. Pete kept up his end of the bargain, and two years later he came home to announce that he was engaged to his girlfriend, Mary Leone. Dad not only refused to honor his promise to Pete, he also kicked him out of the house without giving him a dime. Pete was forced to borrow $25 from Mr. Musselman, the local grocer, to pay for his wedding in Reno, Nevada.

There was also nothing Mama could do when the "gold bug" bit my dad again. She stood by helplessly as he took $1,000 out of the family coffers one day and used it to purchase an interest in the Carr Mine in Northern Butte County. He was back in the mine business again—only this time not as a laborer, but as an investor. My father was convinced that a fabulous "mammoth channel" of gold existed somewhere in the hills near Stirling City, and he was determined to find it. Soon, the Butte County records books were full of mining claims that Dad had filed. Any family money that remained after paying the monthly bills was used for expenses associated with the mining claims. We were "mining poor," as my father's fascination with gold ensured that we never had a penny to spare.

While my father dreamed of instant wealth, my mother was grounded in the realities of the here and now. Our family was completed in 1934, nine years after my birth, when my brother Franklin was born. My father was 53 years of age and my mother was 41 at the time. With three kids still at home, boarders to feed, and a restaurant to run, Mama was a constant whirlwind of activity. As I continued my elementary school years, she still did the washing in a tub, cleaned the bed sheets by boiling them in a big tub over an open fire, and dried clothes by hanging them on a line hooked to a tree. While we still used an outhouse, we could finally claim piped water and an indoor sink.

John and I were given responsibility for the rabbit hutch and making sure that the baby chicks had plenty of wet mash. This was often a very time consuming chore, especially in the winter months when the water containers in the rabbit hutch would freeze solid, and we would have to carry big pots of boiling water to the hutch to help break the ice. John was a diligent worker, but it was clear that his heart was in his classroom studies and not his chores. A gifted student, he told Mama that he wouldn't make all A's if he had to devote so much of his study time to helping care for the rabbits. Ever practical, Mama instructed, "John, you get all the A's. Harry, you do the work." (I couldn't have made all A's if I had studied around the clock, so Mama's instructions seemed like a good deal to me.)

One day, Mama came to John and me and said that she needed our help in feeding the boarders when they had their lunch break at the mill. The moment our school lunch bell rang, she wanted us to run the mile or so between the school and our house, help her serve and clean the dishes, re-fill the wood stove, and then run back to school—arriving before the bell rang to end the lunch hour. John and

I sat there with our mouths open when Mama told us what she wanted us to do. When she was done, I respectfully explained, "Mama, we just can't get here that fast from school, do all the work you need us to do, and then make it back to school before classes start again."

She responded by saying, "If you run real fast, you can." You know what? She was right. John and I had to pick up the pace to make it to home and back to school in time, but we did it day after day. I am an optimist by nature, but there have been times in my career when I questioned whether a job could get done, a task completed, or a challenge overcome. Whenever those times occurred, I could almost hear Mama saying, "If you run real fast, you can." I would then redouble my efforts and invariably reach my goal.

The fact is that I liked to work hard—a trait that was rewarded one day when I was twelve years old. The local grocer, Mr. Musselman, drove to our home to deliver a supply of chicken feed and wheat in 135 pound sacks. I immediately started unloading the sacks from his truck, stacking and organizing them the way Mama had taught me to organize the chicken house—everything was neat, tidy, and in order. Mr. Musselman inspected my work, saw how clean I kept the chicken coop, and told my father that he wished he had a kid like me working for him. "Take him" was Dad's immediate response. Minutes later, I found myself riding back to the mercantile with Mr. Mussleman, where I began work that very day. For the next four years, it would become my second home, as I would spend every afternoon during the school year and from 7:00a.m. to 7:00p.m. during the summers working at the mercantile.

On my first day on the job, Mr. Musselman asked me to clean the store and to fill the shelves. I did that, and then the noon hour arrived and I didn't know that I was supposed to take an hour off for lunch, so I went to the back room that was used for storage and saw that it was a mess. There was a mirror so dirty you couldn't see yourself, and a porcelain sink that was black with grime. Again, I did what I thought Mama would have done. I cleaned everything, and by the time I was through scrubbing, the mirror, the sink, and the floor looked like new. Mr. Musselman's wife happened to drop by the room that afternoon and literally screamed with surprise. "Look what the little Merlo boy has done!" she delightedly told her husband.

It wasn't long before Mr. Musselman had entrusted me to drive his pickup truck nineteen miles up the road to Butte Meadows, where he had opened a smaller store to serve a nearby logging camp. I'd open up that store in the morning, stay until after lunch, take orders for the next day, and then drive the pickup back to the main store in Stirling City, where I would work the rest of the day. At five o'clock the next morning, I'd load all the orders on the pick up and drive them up to the logging camp to begin another day's work. All for the princely salary of a dollar a day. The experience was more than just salary to me, however. It also provided me with an education almost as important as the one I received in the classroom. It was in the mercantile where I learned about banking, finances, salesmanship, and the art of keeping the customer happy.

One lesson occurred when the annual winter snows shut the mill down, and the employees of the mill—all customers of the mercantile—would receive no paychecks and have no money with which to purchase goods. Mr. Musselman told me, "Kid," (he always called me "Kid") "for the next few months you don't have to take money from the customers. Instead, write a ticket for everything they buy, give them one copy of the ticket, and put another copy in the cash register." He explained to me that this was buying on credit, and that when the snows melted and the mill opened back up in the spring, his customers would again be receiving paychecks, and they would then pay their bills in full. I took this all in, and when I returned home that evening, I reported to Mama that we could get all our groceries for nothing by paying with something called "credit." "No thanks," she said. "We will pay with cash." I can't remember Mama ever buying anything on credit.

I also recall that whenever a customer did pay their bill, Mr. Musselman would give them a little "bonus"—usually a piece of candy or a pack of cigarettes. He explained to me that this was just a little extra touch he had designed to gain some good will from his customers, and to ensure that they would continue to pay their bills in full.

I reflected on this lesson a half-century or so later when, as the new CEO of Louisiana-Pacific, I flew into New York City to meet with the bankers who held the $186 million debt owed by L-P. As I exited the airport to hail a cab, I discovered to my surprise that the bankers had sent a limousine to pick me up. Up to that time, I had never ridden a limousine in my life, and on the trip into the city, I pinched myself a time or two and reflected on how far my life's journey had taken me. It was hard to imagine that Harry Merlo from Dago Town, who grew up in a home where every penny mattered, was now owing someone $186 million. I couldn't help but smile and laugh as it dawned on me that the limousine they had sent for me was the equivalent of Mr. Musselman's candy and cigarettes—the bankers were showing me a little good will to win my loyalty and to help ensure that the $186 million loan would be repaid.

During my years in the timber industry, I achieved a reputation as someone who could sell ice cream to Eskimos. While I suppose that I am a good salesman, my years with Mr. Mussleman also led me to conclude that basic common sense has a great deal to do with success in sales. I recall, for instance, the time there was a 25 gallon barrel inside the mercantile that was half-full of prunes which Mr. Musselman was selling for a penny a pound. The problem was that it was very difficult for customers to reach the prunes in this huge barrel, and some of the customers were actually using it as a garbage can, throwing scrap paper and other items on top of the prunes. It was no wonder that prune sales were very low! Common sense suggested to me that sales wouldn't improve until we cleaned up the barrel, and made it easier for the customers to reach the prunes. I turned the barrels upside down, so it could never again be used for customers' trash, and filled a supply of cellophane bags—a new invention at the time--with three pounds of prunes to a bag. I set the bags within easy reaching range on top of and around the barrel, and displayed a sign that read, "3 cents a pound; Limit 2 bags a customer." All the prunes were sold in two days.

Common sense was also important to Mama, who often proclaimed that the two most important qualities for a person to possess were common sense and courage. Mama was very proud of my work at the mercantile, and when I told her one day that I was thinking about asking Mr. Musselman for a small raise to reward the increased duties and responsibilities he continued to assign me, she quickly instructed me to dismiss those thoughts, saying, "Go into your bedroom, get down on your knees, and thank God that you are the only boy in Stirling City to have a job." Mama made it very clear, however, that she did not expect me to work in the mercantile the rest of my life. She urged me to prepare myself so I could eventually hold a "bigger job"—a bank teller, perhaps. Her dream for my brothers and me was that we would one day wear a suit and tie to work, and not do manual labor all our lives.

As my school years continued, I had more immediate concerns on my mind—concerns like the seventy-two mile a day round trip on the school bus to Chico High School; and concerns like staying warm on cold winter nights. Without electricity, the only warmth my siblings and I had on those nights came courtesy of a brick that Mama would warm on the stove, wrap with a towel, and put on the foot of our bed.

Sadly, the warmth I received from that brick exceeded the emotional warmth I received from my father. There were definitely two camps in the Merlo household. Mama and all the children were in one camp. Dad was in the other. My siblings and I lived in fear of Dad, never knowing what would set him off. As we grew taller and stronger, however, my brothers and I would begin to assert a measure of control and would unite to protect our mother.

I think Dad first realized the tide had shifted during an incident that arose from Mama's desire to become a United States citizen. Although Dad had earned his citizenship soon after his arrival in California, he had steadfastly refused to allow Mama take her citizenship test. My brothers and I then decided to help Mama go behind his back. After Dad went to work, Mama would head to the outhouse at 10:00a.m. each morning, where she would devote time to studying for the exam. When she told us she was ready, we all rode the bus to Oroville, where she passed the test with flying colors. When we all returned home that evening, we confessed to Dad what we had done. He immediately went to his and Mama's bedroom, and returned with his shotgun, proclaiming that he was going to kill us for what we had done. For a moment, I thought my brothers and I would be forced to gang up and wrestle the gun away from him. But faced with our united front, he retreated to the bedroom and put his gun away. He would never threaten us again.

My days were so busy with school and work that I usually didn't have time to think about why Dad was so indifferent and abusive to his family, or to dwell on how poor we were. Nights, however, were different. During the cold and dark months of winter I would remain awake in bed, often becoming depressed. Escape from my surroundings would come by dreaming I was Joe DiMaggio hitting a home run for the New York Yankees.

No matter how difficult the situation, Mama retained an unshakable optimism. There were occasions when she even made poverty seem like fun. I recall the time when John was to be honored for his academic achievements at the annual California Boys State gathering in Sacramento. John wanted to look his best when receiving his award—a tough task since the only shoes he owned were so full of holes they could have doubled for Swiss cheese. Since we couldn't afford new shoes, Mama enlisted my help in mixing up a glue mixture of flour and water and plugging the holes with a combination of cardboard and newspapers. It wasn't high fashion, but it worked.

Mama was always thinking of others—especially children, who claimed a special place in her heart. She saved pennies, nickels and dimes in a jar, and two times a year she would cash them in and send a money order to Boys Town in Omaha, Nebraska. "If you never share a dollar, you will never share a million," she observed.

Years later, my brother, Amiel, who was the comedian in the family, would enjoy spinning tall stories about how poor we were. "We were so poor," Amiel would say, "that Dad took us to the graveyard every Christmas Eve to show us where Santa Claus was buried."

"We were so poor," he might add, "that Dad would get me up every morning at 5:00a.m. and make me crow like a rooster, so the neighbors would think we were rich enough to own chickens." (I shared these jokes a few years back at a gathering of the American Academy of Achievement, where I have to admit I was topped by Herschel Walker, the former Heisman Trophy winner and National Football League star running back. Herschel told me that when he was growing up, "his family was so poor that every morning his mother would take him to Kentucky Fried Chicken to lick other people's fingers!")

In February of 1941, during my sophomore year in high school, our meager finances had stabilized enough so that my family moved out of Dago Town and into a house in Stirling City proper. The house was still very small, but it seemed like a castle to me. The move also marked the end of the boarders and the home restaurant. More restaurants had opened up in Chico, and the trip up a dangerous mountain road discouraged customers from making the trip. Mama thought about opening up a restaurant down the road in the larger community of Paradise, but she couldn't find an acceptable location. Later that summer, I thought I could contribute more to the family accounts by making "big money" in the lumber yard. I was offered eighty cents an hour to break down lumber piles for shipment to Chico. Eighty cents an hour! This seemed like a fortune compared to the dollar a day I was making at the mercantile, so after four years of employment with Mr. and Mrs. Musselman, I thanked them and left. On my second day at my new job, I looked up from my work and saw Mr. Anderson, the yard foreman, marching my way with Joe Pittman, a local 18 year old boy and his mother. Mrs. Pittman had complained to Mr. Anderson that it was unfair for him to hire a 16 year old boy like me, when a 18 year old man like her son was in need of work.

While the foreman did not hire Mrs. Pittman's son, he did tell me that he understood her point, and that he would have to let me go.

While I knew that Mr. and Mrs. Musselman would have hired me back in a minute, I had too much pride to go to them and admit I had made a mistake. Besides, I knew it was time for me to venture out. So I went to Susanville, 45 miles away, and worked in the Fruit Growers box factory all that summer. My job was to take boards off the cutting line and sort them by grade in the right piles. It was the furthest I had ever traveled, the first time I had ever been away from home, and it was the loneliest time of my life. I didn't know a soul, and all I'd do is go to work and return to my very small room at night and write Mama a letter. I couldn't wait to return home and to high school that fall.

A few months after my return, on a November Saturday in 1941, I decided to do what I often did on fall Saturdays—go pheasant hunting. Since my brother Pete, who was my usual hunting partner, was unavailable, my brother Amiel, who was not as fond of hunting as Pete and I were, graciously volunteered to accompany me. We were soon off to Orland, a small town in the Sacramento Valley farmland flats. Amiel was driving our Model A when I saw a pheasant and we pulled over to the side of the road. I got out of the car with my shotgun. Amiel was pulling his shotgun out of his side of the car when the car door swung shut and hit the butt of his gun, causing it to discharge. Pellets blasted straight through the car door, hitting me in both legs just above my knees, and ramming a piece of door metal as big as a half dollar in my calf. It hurt like hell.

Amiel was nearly in shock, stammering, "You're going to die, aren't you, Harry?"

"Of course not," I assured him—although I wasn't so sure, as my wounds were bleeding profusely. I knew that if I wanted to live, I would have to save myself, as Amiel, who always fainted at the sight of blood, couldn't even bring himself to look at the wound. I staggered to the car, told Amiel to drive, and we set off to find the nearest doctor or hospitial.

Providentially, I had recently attended my first and only Boy Scout meeting. (When I was two minutes late returning home from the meeting Dad whipped me all the way into the house, and prohibited me from ever attending again.) That meeting had included training on how to prepare and tie a tourniquet. Remembering what I had learned, I used a red handkerchief as a tourniquet for the wound, releasing and retying the handkerchief every 15 minutes to keep the circulation flowing. Unfortunately, every time I released the handkerchief, the blood would literally spurt through my wounds like a high-powered sprinkler. I told Amiel to focus on the road, so he wouldn't pass out while he was behind the wheel.

Eventually, we found a semi-retired doctor who was over 90 years old. He took one look at the leg, and called for an ambulance to run me to the hospital in Chico. He also wanted to give me some morphine to ease the pain. I declined, as I was concerned the morphine would also put me to sleep, and I knew that if I was to survive, I had to remain conscious. The pain and my frustration increased a few miles later when we discovered that the entire causeway was blocked by a flock of some 2,000 sheep very slowly making their way to pasture. We honked and yelled and inched our way through the sheep and down the road. It took us all of three hours to finally reach a hospital, where the emergency room doctor took one look at the wound and announced that my right leg needed amputation. I was stunned with his diagnosis, and told him and anyone who would listen that my leg would not be amputated. I was only 16 years old, and the medical staff wasn't about to listen to me, so they said they would call my parents to receive their approval. I told them that we didn't have a phone, and repeated my refusal to have my leg cut off.

My stand-off with the emergency room doctor continued until the hospital surgeon arrived to see me. I was relieved to finally see a friendly face, as the surgeon, Dr. Lew Ohlker, was the son of the band teacher at Chico High School. Dr. Ohlker had been a star athlete at the University of Southern California, knew of my love of track and field, and understood what amputating my leg would mean to my future. He performed a quick examination, and told me that if I would let him operate on me, he would save my leg and have me back on the track team the next year. I readily agreed, and was quickly placed under anesthetic. When I woke up, I was happy to discover that I was still alive, and relieved that I still had two legs. My recovery was to be lengthy and painful. The wound had to heal from the inside out, so it wasn't stitched and it had to be syringed every day. Each time they did so, the pain was so excruciating it felt like I was being shot all over again.

The incident was also the first—and certainly not the last—time that the press would get the story wrong about me. The *Chico Enterprise* reported that "the youth was shot with a .22 caliber rifle," and that my injuries were only a "flesh wound." In fact, the weapon was a 12 gauge shotgun, and the wound was deep—so deep that, to this day, 92 #4 pellets still remain in my right leg, 15 remain in my left, and occasional surgeries have been needed over the years when a pellet worked its way to the surface.

⚹⚹⚹⚹

CHAPTER 5

Semper Fi

I was still in the hospital on December 7, 1941, when the Japanese bombed Pearl Harbor and World War II began. I continued with my high school education for the next year and half, knowing that when I graduated in June of 1943, I would join most of my other male classmates in entering the military. It was my intention to volunteer for the Navy, where I hoped to serve as a naval aviator. Mama, however, was deathly afraid of airplanes, and tearfully begged me not to be a pilot. She was relieved when I instead decided to volunteer for the Marine Corps, but what she did not realize was that the mortality rates of second lieutenants in the Marine Corps was among the highest of any service. After taking an examination, I received an assignment to the newly created "V-12" Program.

The V-12 program had been initiated just months earlier by the military to meet the need for commissioned officers and to address the concerns of colleges and universities who feared that the flood of young males volunteering and being drafted into the military would leave their classrooms empty. Participants in the V-12 program were from one of three categories: students already enrolled in the Navy and Marine Corps college reserve programs, enlisted men who were recommended by their commanding officers, and high school seniors who, like me, had passed a nationwide qualifying examination.

Participants in this program could not be married and had to agree to remain single until commissioned or released from training. After completing the equivalent of two years college education—crammed into a year and a half—enlistees were next shipped off to boot camp, then to officer candidate school, and finally were placed on general duty. Between 1943 and 1946, over 125,000 men were part of the V-12 program. Included in this group were many who would later gain prominence, including United States Senators Howard Baker of Tennessee, Daniel Patrick Moynihan of New York, and Jeremiah Denton of Alabama; former FBI and CIA Director William Webster, and entertainers Johnny Carson and Jack Lemmon.

Upon entering the program in July 1943, I was placed aboard a train bound for Arizona State Teachers College (now Northern Arizona University) in Flagstaff. This was the first time I had ever traveled beyond the borders of Chico or Susanville. Prior to the military, my whole life had been spent close to family, friends, and Stirling City. Now, my weekdays were spent in classes with fellow recruits from every corner of the country, and weekends included many more hours of studying, along with the occasional dance or trip to the Grand Canyon, located sixty miles north of campus. Whenever I felt especially homesick—and there were plenty of times when I did—I would often drop by a local sawmill just to smell the lumber and to soak in the atmosphere that had been such a constant part of my life.

After two terms in Arizona, I was assigned in February of 1944 to the V-12 Marine College Detachment at Southwestern Louisiana Institute (now the University of Southwestern Louisiana) in Lafayette. The officer in charge urged us "to enter into and engage in extra-curricular activities of all kinds in order to broaden our personalities,

develop leadership, and to teach us how to get along with people."
I did as instructed, marching in war bond parades, giving blood to
the American Red Cross, and participating in any number of athletic
activities, including track and field and boxing. Perhaps the childhood
fights I engaged in when other kids poked fun of my Italian heritage
came in handy, as I soon developed quite a reputation as one of the
best boxers in my detachment.

In fact, a Marine Corps Major came up to me one day, and
barked my name—"Merlo!"

"Yes, Sir!" I replied.

"I hear you are doing a lot of boxing," he said.

"Yes, Sir!" I replied.

"Would you like to enter a tournament and represent the
Marines?" he asked.

"No, Sir!" I replied, as while I enjoyed boxing, I did not like
doing so in front of crowds.

"Are you a marine, Merlo?" asked the Major.

"Yes, Sir!" I replied.

"Then you'll fight! he ordered.

"Yes, Sir!" I replied.

I was soon participating in a light heavyweight boxing tournament
and never lost on my way to the championship bout. I won that fight
with a first round TKO, but, more importantly, the audience for the
evening's activities purchased over $10,000 of war bonds. Assisting
me that night as my "corner man" was a Marine named Alvin Dark,
who would later go on to baseball fame as the Major League Rookie of
the Year in 1948 for the Boston Braves, and would spend many years
as a Major League Baseball manager, guiding the Oakland Athletics to
a World Series victory in 1974.

Everything inside me wanted to be fighting in real combat rather than in a boxing ring, and the next step to reach that goal in our V-12 training was eight weeks of boot camp at Parris Island, South Carolina. Ask any veteran to tell you about boot camp and you are apt to hear it described as one of the most demanding experiences imaginable. While in boot camp, you are cut off entirely from the civilian world and forced to adapt to a Marine Corps lifestyle. Physical fitness is emphasized through hikes and runs, and drill instructors constantly push and challenge recruits by forcing them to perform basic tasks over and over again. I will never forget being rousted out of bed at 2:00 a.m. and being ordered to run around the barracks buck naked while holding buckets of sand. We were then ordered to stand at attention for hours on end. If the heat and humidity didn't get to you once the sun came up, the sand fleas ate you alive. If anyone moved to swat a sand flea or to scratch a bite, then ten more minutes of standing at attention was added.

I also recall one occurrence when my unit was participating in a 10 mile hike. The military had strict rules for every activity, and the regulations for 10 mile hikes stated that you should pack an extra pair of boots in your backpack. I did so, and when we reached the half-way point of the hike, the Drill Instructor ordered us to take off the boots we were wearing and to put on the ones in our backpacks. As I began to do so, I realized that I was the only member of my platoon who had actually packed the required extra pair of boots. Not wanting to set myself apart from the team, I quickly returned the extra boots to the backpack, and joined my fellow soldiers in walking the rest of the hike in our stocking feet.

Exercises like these were designed to instill camaraderie and teamwork, and no one wanted to let their fellow soldiers down by failing or dropping out of a task. Those who flunked out of V-12 training also faced the pressure of knowing that exiting the program meant a quick transfer to the front lines. More than once, I would return to barracks to find that a good friend had failed the training, and that he had been shipped out without a chance to say farewell.

I managed to survive boot camp, and was then sent to officer's school in Quantico, Virginia, where, in early 1945, at the age of 19, I was officially commissioned as a Second Lieutenant in the United States Marine Corps.

I had been in the military for eighteen months, and still hadn't left stateside or seen real combat. With my training complete and my commission in hand, I was sure that I would soon have the opportunity to fight for my country, and was excited when I was sent to Camp Pendleton in Southern California, as that was a major staging point for troops being sent to combat.

The tide had turned in the European theater, and Germany was just months away from surrendering. While the war was also going America's way in the Pacific, everyone expected that Japan would fight to the last man. In preparation for leaving for the Pacific theater, my platoon participated in a landing simulation that involved jumping off landing crafts and running to the beach. I was making my way to shore when a 30 caliber machine gun carried by one of the enlisted men in my unit fell on my leg—the same leg I had injured in the hunting accident—and put me in the hospital. Fortunately, the leg was not broken, but the muscles and tendons were torn and would take months to heal. By the time I could get up and hobble around, the war was over.

I have always regretted the fact that I never was able to go into combat, but I also look back at my years in the Marine Corps as one of the best and most valuable experiences of my life. The Marine Corps expanded my horizons both figuratively and literally. It was here where I truly saw the critical importance of common sense and courage—the qualities that Mama had spoken about so often. It was in the Marine Corps where I also received my first taste of leadership, learning how to rapidly size up situations, how to take decisive action, and how to earn the respect and trust of members of your team—lessons that would prove very useful during my years as corporate leader.

✝✝✝✝

Home from the war, four for four.
I'm in the front. In the back from left to right are John, Frank, Amiel and Pete.

✝✝✝✝

CHAPTER 6

From Calfskins to College

WHILE STILL IN THE HOSPITAL recovering from the injuries sustained at Camp Pendleton, I desperately searched for activities to keep me from boredom. One day I poked my head in the occupational therapy wing, and discovered a free supply of 10,000 calfskins, in every color. It has been my experience that opportunity doesn't just knock once—it knocks regularly —but sometimes it is unrecognizable as it resembles hard work. I concluded that 10,000 free calfskins presented me with an opportunity that I couldn't pass up.

There was apparently an artistic gene in me somewhere, and after some minimal training I started hand tooling leather wallets, embossing them with a likeness of a dog, trout, duck, or pheasant. I gave my first efforts away to friends, relatives, and other patients in the hospital, but when I saw their positive reaction to the wallets, it also dawned on me that they might have some commercial potential. I began to produce as many wallets as I could—my record was 144 in one day—selling them at a price of $4.00 per wallet. Sales were brisk and I soon needed help to keep up with the orders. I thought the nurses on night shift might be able to stitch wallets during their free time and breaks, and offered them fifty cents per wallet to do so. I also paid corpsmen fifty cents per wallet to sell them around the base. Sales increased even more when a shop in nearby Oceanside,

California ordered enough wallets to turn what started out as a hobby into something that was close to a full-time job.

As my recovery neared completion, I also pondered the possibility of remaining in the Marine Corps. My superiors had rewarded me with high marks, and made it clear that if I would remain in the service, I would be promoted to captain. Mama urged me to remain in the military, and, without actually saying he was proud of me, my father let me know he agreed, as when I returned home to Stirling City for a visit, he would ask me to put my uniform on before I went to town to pick up the mail. Any thoughts that Dad might be softening went out the window when I brought a military buddy home with me one weekend, and Dad actually gave me a bill, demanding reimbursement for the Post Toasties we ate for breakfast!

I was very close to making a decision to remain in the military— a decision that would have certainly altered the path of my life—when an incident occurred that changed my mind. After fully recovering from my leg injury, I was assigned to historic Mare Island Naval Yard near San Francisco, where my duties included supervising a detail of Marine guards. On one occasion, my detail stood outside on duty for many hours in very bad weather, and as the 2:00a.m. time for dinner drew near, I noticed that the meal the cook had prepared for them was a sandwich comprised of two pieces of soggy white bread, peanut butter and lettuce. Seeing just how hungry and tired my men were, I relieved the detail, and took them to the mess hall, where I asked the mess sergeant to supply them with a decent hot meal.

I was called into the Major's office the next morning, where he delivered a stern reprimand, saying I had caused a great deal of trouble, and that the peanut butter and lettuce sandwiches "would not have harmed those men." I thanked the Major for his time, and told him he had just helped me make a big decision. "What decision is that?" the Major asked. "As soon as you dismiss me from this meeting, I am resigning from the Marine Corps," I responded. I concluded by telling him that I thought my job was to take care of my people, and if I didn't have the authority to do that, then I didn't belong in the military. Realizing he had stepped over the line, the Major made an attempt to get me to change my mind, and called in several of his superiors in the effort. I remained firm in my decision, and turned my attention to a future outside of the military.

Ironically, another of my superiors in the Marine Corps, Major George Baker, had a proposal for my next step. Impressed with my wallets, he came to me with the suggestion that I move to his hometown of Cherokee, Iowa, and that we become partners in a wallet business. Since I had no other plans in the works, the idea intrigued me. I wrote to my brother, John, who was also in the process of receiving his discharge from the military, told him of the offer, and invited him to join our new business until he enrolled in college in the fall. He accepted the invitation, and my brother, Pete, who was working at Chico Wood Products, agreed to lend us five thousand dollars so we could purchase our own supply of leather and tools.

Prior to leaving for Iowa, I spent as much time with Mama as I could. It was more obvious than ever to me that my parents' marriage of convenience had never evolved—and would never evolve--into a marriage of love. When I had returned to Stirling City after my military discharge, I was angered to see and to learn that my father's emotional cruelty to Mama had increased. He had refused to buy her any new clothes or material to make dresses, so she had to make due with clothes that were old and torn. My siblings and I agreed that Mama would be better off without Dad. While they were to legally remain husband and wife until Mama's death in 1962, they lived apart from each other for most of the last fifteen years of her life.

I arrived in Iowa in April of 1946, and the BakMer Company, purveyors of fine wallets, key chains, and small leather goods was soon up and running—although it wasn't running very fast. The supply of leather was still controlled by the Office of Price Administration that had been established during the war. As a result, we were only able to receive a few small shipments of leather—not nearly enough to produce the inventory we needed to make a go of it. Then it turned out that the funds that Major Baker had promised to invest in our new business did not really exist. And while Cherokee was full of good people—some who would become my lifelong friends—it was a small town far removed from a major metropolitan area, and was not a venue that would allow us to reach a wide market.

It only took a few months for me to realize that long term success was not in the cards. I told John that he should continue with our plan for him to return west in September so he could take advantage of the GI Bill and enter the University of California at Berkeley. I would remain in Iowa until the end of the year so I could take advantage of the Christmas market and make enough money to pay Pete back the $5,000 he had loaned us. When that was accomplished, I closed up the business, and joined John in January as a student at the university.

With two years of college credit under my belt from the V-12 Marine College detachment, I entered the University of California as a junior, majoring in business administration. I was ambitious enough to believe that I was destined for business success, but in what business? As I searched for that answer, I enrolled in a wide array of classes—management and administration, accounting, marketing, finance, industrial engineering, and inventory management.

This time was one of the happiest of my life. The classes were interesting, and I was back near my family, as Mama and thirteen-year-old Frank moved to Oakland, so she could be near John and me. She cleaned our house, fixed our meals, and instead of spending thirty cents a day on bus fare, she walked thirty-six blocks to her job as a cook at a café. We were united in the desire to prove that we didn't need Dad, so we all took part-time jobs to help make ends meet. I worked on construction crews, John worked at Sears, and Frank had a paper route. (Maybe the muscles Frank earned from riding his bike on the paper route helped make him a tremendous athlete, as he played on the varsity baseball team at the University of California.) Within a year, we were able to amass $1,000 in savings—a pretty impressive figure for the time.

During the summers of 1947 and 1948 I returned to what I knew best—lumber—and worked at Chico Forest Products, where Amiel had worked his way up to a position as bonded warehouseman and production manager. (During his long career in the forest products industry, Amiel would earn a well deserved reputation as a tremendously gifted professional. The intricate moldings and door and window parts he created from sheets of wood were true works of art. Indeed, when I was CEO of L-P and in the midst of spending $41 million to acquire a company that specialized in millwork, my staff advised me to only make the purchase if we could hire Amiel to oversee the millwork operations. Based on their recommendation, I called Amiel and offered him a job, with a salary of $36,000 along with options for 5,000 shares of stock. Amiel told me that my offer was too generous, and he would only accept a salary of $30,000 a year!)

Two years passed very quickly, and in January 1949 I earned my Bachelor of Science in Business Administration, which entitled me to receive my degree in June, when President Harry Truman would be personally handing out the diplomas. I drove through much of Northern California looking for a full-time job, but employment was hard to come by, given the glut of returning veterans that employers could choose from. Since I had not exhausted all my GI Bill benefits, I decided to remain in Berkeley and enrolled in the Master of Business Administration program. When summer rolled around, however, I was back at Chico Forest Products, where I worked in the molding plant. I would also arrive at work two hours early and stay two hours late to pick up extra money piling lumber. I could not afford to leave that behind for a day to go to Berkeley to receive my diploma, regardless of who was handing them out. I decided the "other Harry" would have to get along without me.

As the school year started up again, I found that I needed a job to help pay for rent, food, and the college expenses not covered by my GI benefits. It was slow going, but I finally found a job operating a salvage sawmill for the Cleveland Wrecking Company on San Francisco's waterfront. The nature of the business was perhaps best described in their quarter-page advertisement in the 1949 San Francisco Yellow Pages:

> "If responsibility counts, call Cleveland Wrecking Company. World's biggest wrecking contractors…We have wrecked more buildings than any other firm in the world…. Structures dismantled anywhere, also concrete breaking, grading, excavating. No job too large or too small. We wreck anything from bungalows to office buildings."

My job was to take materials from demolished buildings into a yard, run a metal detector over the salvaged timber, and take the nails out, so that the timber could be milled into saleable lumber. While the job paid the bills, it was not what I wanted to do as a career. And as 1949 drew to an end, I was itching to get on with the rest of my life. While Mama had taught me to always finish what I started, I was tired of the MBA program. It wasn't that the classes weren't interesting, it was just that I was approaching 25 years of age, and I was ready to make my mark. In December 1949 I dropped by the San Francisco office of Rockport Redwood Company to inquire about job openings. The sales manager told me that there were no jobs available, but a representative from the California Redwood Association, who happened to be visiting the office, took me aside and told me that the Rounds and Kilpatrick timber operation in Cloverdale, California was in need of a shipping clerk. On hearing this piece of news, I literally ran to my brown Chevrolet and drove up Highway 101 to Cloverdale.

✮✮✮✮

CHAPTER 7

Shaking My Job to Pieces

As I drove into Cloverdale, located about ninety miles north of San Francisco, I couldn't help but smile, as the community was surrounded by redwood covered hills, and was in the heart of California's wine country. Trees and wine were two constants of my youth, and I felt instantly at home.

My first stop was the Rounds and Kilpatrick Lumber Company, where, after a brief interview, general manager John Rhoda offered me the job of the company's new shipping clerk with a salary of $350 a month. I immediately accepted the offer, and quickly began to make a mental list of what I would need to do to move to Cloverdale from Berkeley. As my new boss gave me a tour of the operation, he also briefed me on its history, size and scope: The company was headed by Ralph Rounds, a successful lumberman from Wichita, Kansas, who expanded his father's midwest lumber business to California in 1937. A little over a decade later, the Rounds' empire was truly impressive, consisting of eight distribution yards and twenty-seven retail yards in the midwest, and four intertwining California companies that provided lumber to a midwest distribution center.

The Cloverdale operation sat on 45 acres of land, and carried an inventory of about fifteen million board feet of Coast Redwood lumber. (Smaller than the better-known Giant Sequoia, which have long been protected from logging, the Coast Redwood produces a high grade of lumber of great durability, strength and appearance.) Rhoda told me that the goal for the coming year was to ship about two and a half million board feet of lumber each month. Some of this was sold to the Morgan Wood Casket Company, which was located just a few hundred yards away, but 80% of what the company produced was shipped by rail to midwest and eastern markets. Fresh cut redwood lumber would arrive at the company for processing and it would be stacked in the yard to air dry. From there, the lumber would be dried in a kiln, and would then enter the remanufacturing plant, where it would be processed according to the specifications of customers. As Rhoda explained the responsibilities of my job, I realized with growing satisfaction that I understood everything he was saying. I had, after all, been born and raised in a lumber yard.

At the end of the tour, Mr. Rhoda asked me if I played baseball. I wasn't surprised by this question, as I knew that fast-pitch softball enjoyed a position of honor in the California timber industry of the 1950's. Every company with enough men fielded a team, and the larger companies were rumored to pad their rosters by hiring professional players who had no other duties besides playing softball. In fact, the manager of the Rounds and Kilpatrick team was Carl Holling, a foreman at the mill who had pitched for the Detroit Tigers in the American League for three years. I told him of my love of baseball and the fact that I had played for a community team during my time in Iowa, and he quickly added me to the roster.

My next step was to find a place to live, and I rented a small street level apartment in an old two-story home for ten dollars a month. The apartment consisted of a table and two chairs, a bunk bed, a hot plate, a bathroom, a telephone, and not much else. I planned on being in the apartment only when I was sleeping, and devoting my waking hours to my new job.

General Manager John Rhoda was a civic-minded man, devoted to his church, active in the local Rotary, and in charge of Cloverdale's annual civic festival. If the community needed something done, he could be counted on to do it. When John had to take a long lunch or a little time away, he began to ask me to watch over the plant. As the months went by, I got the knack of every machine, every work station, every stack of redwood in the yard and in the dry shed. I knew every co-worker as a friend. The rhythm of the plant—sales orders coming in from the sales office in San Francisco, the lumber flowing through on fork lifts, the problem areas, and the solutions to those problems—all seeped into my bones.

I worked around the clock, taking breaks on the weekends, when I would often make the four hour drive to Chico, where Pete and Amiel were working, and where mother and Frank had moved after I graduated from college. During one summer, I brought Frank back to Cloverdale with me and found him a job at the local Chrysler dealership washing cars. Frank took the top bunk, and I took the lower one.

In August of 1950, Mr. Rounds made his semi-annual visit to his west coast operations. It was my first opportunity to meet him, and I confess to being a little in awe. He was the first millionaire I had rubbed elbows with, and I took careful note of how he dressed, how he talked, and how he interacted with his employees. He returned to Cloverdale a few months later for another visit, and this time I got the distinct impression that the tables had turned and that I was the one under the microscope. John Rhoda had confided in him that I was emerging as his second in command, and Mr. Rounds wanted to make sure that John's judgment was correct.

During his next visit to Cloverdale a few months later, Mr. Rounds called me aside and said that he had decided to tell all his midwest managers that they should bypass the larger San Francisco office and go directly to me should they have any inquiries about an order. "I'm confident you can get them a fast answer, Harry," he told me. My phone was soon ringing off the hook as managers called with countless questions and requests. As a result, my voice became familiar to hundreds of lumber wholesalers and retailers in the Rounds operation.

I enjoyed my job immensely, and felt that if John Rhoda were ever to leave or retire, I would be the logical choice to run the Cloverdale operation. Mr. Rounds had other plans, however. In April of 1952 he told me that company profits were not as strong as he had hoped, and he was making some changes in all his companies. He asked if I would move to San Francisco, where I would spend all my time in sales. I told him that I would do anything he asked me to do, but that I felt my highest value was to remain in Cloverdale. He stressed that it was important for company sales to increase, and he thought I was the man who could make that happen. He asked me to try it for a while, and that he would send me back to Cloverdale if I didn't like it.

I packed up my car once again and headed the 90 miles south back to San Francisco. It was a road I was to know very well, as I discovered that my connections to the Cloverdale plant were key to succeeding in my new job. If a sale was dependent on an expedited delivery of lumber, I would race back to Cloverdale to ask the plant crew if they could make it happen. They never let me down. One of the actions I took to secure and win the loyalty of our customers— and to set ourselves apart from our competitors—was to include a case of Italian Swiss Colony wine in every car of lumber. Now, you might think that a $5.00 case of wine in a lumber order that might total many thousand dollars would not be noticed—but you would be wrong. If we forgot to include the wine in a car load, then my phone would soon ring and the customer would demand to know why it wasn't there. Going the extra mile for our customers led to an increase in sales, and Mr. Rounds soon promoted me to sales manager.

I stepped into my new job by taking a six-week trip throughout the midwest and the Atlantic seaboard, with particular emphasis on several big customers in Chicago and New York City. The Rounds operation was smaller than most of our competitors, and I wanted to send the message that despite our size, we were a strong company with a superior product. I was both optimistic and honest—two qualities that are key to succeeding in sales--in making the case that we had a good long-term supply of timber, and that we were here to stay. I followed that trip up with a two-week swing through the south to share the same message. It was a message that hit home, as sales continued to increase, and I was soon promoted to Vice President of Sales for Rounds Lumber Company. As a vice-president, I was considered an officer of the company, and, for the first time, I would have the privilege of attending meetings of the company board of directors.

Reverend Norman Vincent Peale, who became a household name in America in the 1950's through his inspirational television show, once offered this advice: "Think enthusiastically about everything; but especially about your job. If you do so, you'll put a touch of glory in your life. If you love your job with enthusiasm, you'll shake it to pieces." To be involved in the timber industry in California in the 1950's was to "shake your job to pieces." America was growing, and no state was fueling that growth more than California. The industry was full of hard working and colorful personalities with big ambitions, big hearts, and big egos, and many would become my life long friends. There was often bitter competition between companies, but there was also a great deal of camaraderie. We worked together, we played softball together, and we socialized together at meetings and parties of the International Concatenated Order of Hoo-Hoo, the famous fraternal order and service organization for employees of the forest products industry. (During initiation into the organization, new members were instructed to place their right hand over their heart and their left on their "hoo-hoo." After a few embarrassing moments of confusion, the rookies were instructed that the "hoo-hoo" was their head.)

To be sure, the environmental and safety standards of the 1950's were not those that have developed over the ensuing decades. The hours were often long and the work was tough—especially for those in the forests and in the mill—but everyone knew they were involved in an industry that was providing homes to families—an industry that was helping people achieve the American dream.

It was also during this time when I met a wonderful woman who I was certain was the girl of my dreams. Lumber advertising in the 1950's tended to feature beautiful women, and part of my job (one of the best parts!) was the approval of models selected by our advertising agency. One of the models I met was Sheila Murphy, who was the reigning Miss Wisconsin, having competed in the 1952 Miss America pageant, and who was freelancing as a model in San Francisco. We fell hard for each other, and were married on July 3, 1954 at St. Mary's Cathedral in San Francisco. We honeymooned one week at Yosemite National Park, and one week in the Sierras near my childhood stomping grounds. We returned to a home I had purchased shortly before our marriage in the community of Tiburon, across the San Francisco Bay. One of our first purchases as husband

and wife was a Chevrolet station wagon that we hoped and planned to fill with children.

As the years went by, my friendship with Mr. Rounds became almost that of a father and son. He continued to increase my responsibilities, and in 1958, at the age of 33, I became vice president and general manager of Rounds and Kilpatrick. My duties included running the sales office in San Francisco, and running the remanufacturing plant in Cloverdale, where I started my career in the Rounds empire eight years earlier.

The new responsibilities meant more meetings, more hours working late in the office, more trips to company headquarters in Wichita, and much more time in Cloverdale away from home and from Sheila. That, coupled with the fact that all our efforts had not resulted in Sheila becoming pregnant, put strains on our marriage. Since I was spending the majority of my time in Cloverdale, I thought bringing Sheila there would ease those strains. In the fall of 1958, I purchased a ranch on Warm Springs Creek in the Coast Range mountains above Cloverdale. The ranch included green meadows draping the shoulders of rounded hills, oak groves clustering among the ridge tops, redwood shaded ravines, and a shack of a house with no two walls leaning in the same direction. I thought it was as close to Eden as could be found on this earth—and all for $25,000. When it came time to close the sale, the previous owner even threw in his herd of sheep. Since the only experience I had with sheep was navigating through a flock on my way to the hospital after being shot, I made a quick visit to the public library in Cloverdale to check out a book on their care and feeding.

I may not have known how to take care of sheep, but I had learned a thing or two over the years on how to take care of employees. From the time I was a boy in Stirling City through my years in the military to my climb up the ladder in the Rounds empire, I had seen or served under many managers and leaders. I knew from experience how it felt to be trusted and respected by your boss. I knew what it was like to be part of a team. I knew the boredom inherent in mill work, where an operator might spend a lifetime tending one machine all day, every day. As I took charge in Cloverdale, I tried to acknowledge every employee with whom I crossed paths. I would ask them not just about their job, but about their family, as well. My name was Harry—Mr. Merlo was my father. I began cross-training every employee possible to operate more than one machine and to do more than one kind of job. I joined them in competing on our company team on the baseball diamond and at the bowling alley. I installed a new company lunch room with a big kitchen. And if I ever needed anyone to work on a weekend or on Christmas or New Year's Day, then they knew that I would be working right alongside them. I established a tradition of a company spaghetti feed and cooked the big pot of noodles myself. As I hoped, these efforts paid off with a new sense of loyalty in the Cloverdale workforce.

It was a bit of surprise, however, when, just a few months after I took the helm at Cloverdale, Mr. Rounds also put me in charge of part of his timber operation. The redwood timber business consisted of buying stands of uncut trees; the redwood lumber business consisted of manufacturing, selling and shipping a finished product; and the two were very different beasts. The timber business was much more chancy, as when you were buying timber, you were also crossing your fingers that the price you were paying would justify itself by the time logging and saw milling sent the resulting lumber to market. While a lumber salesman often made deals dressed in a sports jacket and necktie, there was no such thing as a timber salesman, and those who bought and sold timber were more than likely to wear mechanic's overalls and a faded shirt. The only necktie they owned was worn when somebody died and they needed to show respect at the funeral. I would venture to guess that more timber was sold in bars and taverns than in any office. It was not uncommon for lawyers going through company files to ask a mill owner what the scribble on a cocktail napkin meant, and receive the reply that it was a timber deal worth $250,000. Experienced lawyers and accountants in the redwood region came to realize they were lucky to have a scribbled napkin, as the only evidence of some deals was a handshake. It was a business where friendships meant a great deal and where a man's word was his bond, and I enjoyed it immensely.

One of the challenges inherent in the timber and lumber industries is that they are very susceptible to cycles of booms and busts, and the year 1960 brought a bust. Residential and industrial construction fell off dramatically. Numerous sawmill and wholesale lumber companies failed. Price competition was more severe than it had ever been and the volume of shipments at Cloverdale dropped nearly 15%. Faced with similar sales figures, other mills had resorted to mass layoffs. I hung on to my crew, taking personnel from departments that weren't busy and doubling them up with a night shift in a department that was busy. This was only possible because I had taken the trouble to cross-train our employees to perform different jobs in the plant.

I was watching the bottom line carefully to ensure that we would survive the tough times when Ralph Rounds died suddenly at the age of 69 on July 23, 1960. Ownership of his empire passed to his two sons, Bill and Dwight. Ralph Rounds had taken a chance on me, and had constantly moved me up the corporate ladder, giving me new responsibilities and challenges at every rung. His death hit me very hard, as did news on the home front. After seeing more doctors, Sheila concluded that she would never be able to have children, and she decided to rebuild her modeling career full time. Moreover, she decided to rebuild it in Paris, France. Sheila told me that since I would be in Cloverdale and she would be in Paris, it made sense if we were to get a divorce. I was devastated. Yes, I knew we were having problems, but I was confident we could work them out. I never dreamed we would ever get divorced. I told Sheila I loved her and wanted to save the marriage, and she left open a small window of hope. She replied that she would think about a reconciliation—but only after she made it on her own as a model.

I was still grieving from the death of Mr. Rounds and the apparent failure of my marriage when I learned that a fire had devastated the Crofoot Lumber Company, which was the number one supplier of lumber for the Cloverdale mill. All my attention immediately turned to finding replacement suppliers so that we could continue to meet our orders. I had been accustomed to long days, but I made them even longer as I tried to deal with the bad news that seemed to be coming from all directions. I prided myself on staying in top physical shape, but the emotional drain of personal and professional problems placed my resistance on rock bottom, and while in San Francisco, I came down with a horrible case of the mumps. I ended up stuck in a hotel for two weeks—and room service and housekeeping refused to enter because I was contagious. Eventually, my brother Frank came to visit, and alarmed by my condition, he arranged for a private nurse he knew to come to the hotel to take care of me. A few nights later, Dwight Rounds came to my room to bring me some dinner and to talk business. Business turned to pleasure for Dwight, as he fell in love at first sight with my nurse. They were married not long after they met in my hotel room.

The financial situation of Rounds and Kilpatrick began to improve in 1962 as the ebb and flow of the lumber market would again turn favorable. On a personal level, however, it was to be a very tough year. In August, Mama came for an extended visit to the ranch. During that visit, she insisted on cooking a special Sunday night dinner for my brother, Pete; his wife, Leone; their sons, Roger and Ralph; and a group of our friends from San Francisco who had all come to the ranch for a weekend hunting trip. Her cooking was still amazing, and she delighted in our compliments. When she awoke the next morning, she came out to the kitchen, said that she wasn't feeling well, and went back to bed. When I went to check on her a little bit later, I noticed that Mama's breathing seemed labored, and immediately called the doctor. By the time the doctor arrived, it was too late. Mama was in a coma, and she died within the hour.

I suppose that Mama's story was not unique. After all, countless thousands of Italians immigrated to America in the early part of the 20th century and went on to lead productive lives. Mama, however, was truly one of a kind. She was the most selfless and hardest working individual I have ever known. Any successes I have achieved would not have occurred without the example of common sense and courage she set, the lessons she taught, and the sacrifices she made.

My father would outlive my mother by eighteen years, as he passed away in 1980 at 99 years of age. While I never claimed to understand his behavior and the lack of affection and attention he gave to Mama and his children, my brothers and I kept in contact with Dad, and made sure that his final years were comfortable ones.

⚓⚓⚓⚓

⚓⚓⚓⚓

CHAPTER 8

Up the Ladder

IT TOOK A WHILE TO get used to the fact that Mama was gone. More than once, I caught myself wanting to pick up the phone to call and tell her something interesting that had happened in my day. And one thing you could count on in the timber industry is that there was always something interesting happening, always a new challenge to overcome.

Some of the challenges came from Mother Nature. Just as farmers are often dependent on the whims of the weather, so, too, is the timber industry. There was little I could do when fires caused by lightning strikes would destroy countless acres of timber. And there was little I could do when the 1964 "flood of a century" devastated California's north coast. The single track of the Northwest Pacific Railroad serving the "redwood empire" was washed out in so many places it took six months to put it back in operation. Highway 101 remained impassible for three months. Getting lumber to our customers and logs to our mills was nearly impossible. Indeed, for many people, just getting to work was impossible.

The biggest professional challenge for me in the 1960's, however, was the fact that I was simply not challenged enough—and, more importantly, the employees I managed were not challenged enough. There were many instances when I proposed expansions or put together deals that I believed would make the entire Rounds empire bigger and better. These proposals were routinely turned down, as Bill and Dwight Rounds gave every indication that they were perfectly satisfied with the size of the business, and saw no need to grow it or to take actions that would lead to greater profits.

Despite my frustrations, I was not actively looking for a new job. After all, the Rounds organization had taken a chance on me, and had moved me up the corporate ladder, entrusting me at every step of the way with increased responsibilities.

My responsibilities were also increasing outside the office as well. Sheila and I had eventually divorced, and I had begun to date a lovely woman named Nadine Purdy. Nadine was raising a son and a daughter from her previous marriage, and I quickly became very attached to Bill and Andrea, as well. Nadine accepted my proposal of marriage, and our family would be complete in 1967 with the birth of our son, Harry, Jr.

I also found time to become involved in the California Redwood Association, which was one of California's leading timber industry organizations. My fellow association members honored me in 1966 by electing me President of the CRA. My first goal was to search for ways in which the industry could find common ground with the rapidly expanding environmental movement. Although there were over 80 state and county parks in California containing countless acres of redwoods that were protected from harvesting, the environmental community and some in the national media wanted to expand the protected acreage with the creation of a massive new Redwood National Park. I understood that there were additional acres worthy of protection, but believed that locking up as many acres as some were proposing would put many timber companies out of business, and thousands of their employees out of a job.

It was my hope to broker a compromise, and I gathered industry leaders and proposed that each timber company in the CRA should sell a certain percentage of their holdings—something in the 10-15% range—to the government to be used as parklands protected from logging. It was too much for most of the other leaders of the CRA, who voted down my proposal. One industry giant who was intrigued by the idea, however, was the man who was to play such an important role in my future, Robert Pamplin, Sr., Chief Executive Officer of Georgia-Pacific.

A soft-spoken and courtly native of Virginia, Pamplin spent his early years on a small family farm and graduated from Virginia Tech University in the midst of the depression. Jobs were tough to find, but Pamplin was finally offered one by Owen Cheatham, who was the brother of his college roommate. Cheatham was the owner of Georgia Hardwood Company, a small company of four employees in Augusta, Georgia. When Pamplin was hired, the company had annual sales of around $200,000. By the time Pamplin became president of the company in 1957—which had by then changed its name to Georgia-Pacific—sales figures had increased to $120 million annually. By the mid 1960's, it was the largest and most respected forest products company in America.

My duties at Rounds and Kilpatrick had led to many interactions with Georgia-Pacific, as on numerous occasions I had purchased timber from them for our mill in Carlota, California. The year after the California Redwood Association meeting, Rounds and Kilpatrick was again in need of timber, and I again looked to Georgia-Pacific. The purchase price of the timber under our most recent contract was $30 per thousand board feet. I was stunned, then, that the price I was quoted for a new contract was more than double that—$65 per thousand board feet. Since we needed 30 million board feet to meet our orders, that meant a total purchase price of $1,950,000. It was a big amount, but I didn't have much of a choice, as we needed the timber and no one else was offering that much for sale.

A year later, as I was preparing to again buy timber from Georgia-Pacific, I sent Mr. Pamplin our operating statement and balance sheet as a courtesy. Upon receipt of this information, he called me and posed the following question in his southern accent: "Harry, how are you making so much money? You cut 30 million board feet of timber, on which we charge you $65 per thousand board feet, and G-P cuts 100 million board feet of timber, which costs us only $12 per thousand board feet, and you still make more money than we do. How do y'all do that?" I respectfully told him that was my business.

Robert B. Pamplin Sr.

He was silent for a moment, and then he took me by surprise by asking if I would consider coming to work at Georgia-Pacific as one of his vice presidents. I explained that my loyalty to the Rounds family prevented me from accepting, and also told him that G-P already had so many vice-presidents, he couldn't count them all. Mr. Pamplin then upped the ante, saying that if it took buying the entire Rounds operation for me to work for him, then he was willing to do just that. He also promised that I would report directly to him and to no one else. He ended the call by asking me to talk to the appropriate people to determine if there was interest in selling the company and to get back to him as soon as possible with a price.

Still somewhat in shock, I quickly called Dwight and Bill Rounds in Wichita to relay Pamplin's offer. They were very interested, and the next day I called Mr. Pamplin to tell him that Rounds and Kilpatrick was for sale for $4,750,000. "That's fine, Harry," he said. "When can you start working for me?" "I'm working right now," I responded, and I insisted that he come to Cloverdale to see what he was buying. I told him, "We are very proud of what we've done and I won't close the deal until you see it first."

Mr. Pamplin flew down the next day to Cloverdale, and I accompanied him on his tour of our plant there and our sawmill in Carlota. As I knew he would be, he was very impressed with the cleanliness and organization of our facilities, and the talents and work ethic of our employees.

After the tour, Mr. Pamplin and I went to lunch where I had a glass of red wine to help celebrate our deal. He looked a bit shocked, and informed me that at Georgia-Pacific no one could drink wine at lunch unless they took the afternoon off, as they would not be fit to work. He was stunned when I told him that under those conditions, he couldn't buy Rounds and Kilpatrick. When he asked for an explanation, I said, "Remember that nice employee lunch room you complimented me on? Well, I would estimate that over half of those lunch buckets contain a thermos full of red wine. In fact, I started drinking a glass of ½ wine and ½ water with my meals at the age of five, and I've been doing so ever since." Mr. Pamplin thought quietly for a moment and then said, "Well, Harry, maybe that's alright then!" With that, the deal was solidified.

There were, however, a few hiccups in the negotiation process that would lead to the final contract. Rounds and Kilpatrick controlled about 7% of the redwood market, while Georgia-Pacific controlled approximately 15%. The proposed buyout would give GP 22% of the redwood market, which, under anti-trust law, might constitute an illegal monopoly. It took several months for the Federal Trade Commission to examine the buyout and to give its approval. The final roadblock involved my salary. The compensation I was receiving at Rounds and Kilpatrick was greater than the salaries made by other vice-presidents at Georgia-Pacific. I knew that accepting a job running an entire corporate division with thousands of employees at a salary that was substantially less than I had previously been paid would compromise my credibility as an executive.

Pamplin understood my concerns but said that his board of directors simply would not let him pay me more than all the other vice-presidents. Instead of more money, he offered me some options on Georgia-Pacific stock and his personal guarantee that he would find some way to ensure that my compensation would be greater than it had been at Rounds and Kilpatrick. Some in my position might have demanded a written agreement containing Mr. Pamplin's promise. I did not. I knew he was a gentleman and his word was his bond. And so on May 1 1967, I reported to work as vice president in charge of timber, plywood, and lumber operations in the Samoa, California division of Georgia-Pacific.

The town of Samoa was built in 1892 by a group of investors from Eureka, California. The 270 acre tract was built on a peninsula with a mile of waterfront on two sides—the Pacific Ocean on the west, and Humboldt Bay on the east. The investors named their town site after the South Pacific island because the word "Samoa" had been made famous at that time by sensational front-page newspaper coverage of tribal wars. When I arrived 75 years after the town was founded, Samoa was known throughout the timber industry as the site of a huge Georgia-Pacific industrial operation that included a log yard, a redwood sawmill, a stud mill, a plywood plant, a warehouse, shipping docks, lumber drying yards, and a new pulp mill with a mountainous chip pile that received its nickname "Diamond Head" because it resembled Honolulu's famous volcano. The buildings comprising the town of Samoa were also largely owned by Georgia-Pacific, and many homes and neighborhoods had been allowed to fall into disrepair.

My first goal during my initial days in Samoa was to personally meet as many of the 1,500 employees as possible. I had met many of the supervisors during my years in the industry, but I was unknown to the vast majority of employees. If I was to have the confidence of my co-workers, I didn't want to remain unknown for long. I set about to walk through every corner of the operation, shaking hands, looking people in the eye, learning their names and telling them that "Mr. Merlo was my father" and they should call me Harry," and asking for their ideas and suggestions on ways to improve the facility.

If my first goal was to earn the respect of the employees I was to manage, my second goal was to have those employees respect each other and the community in which they lived. On my second day on the job, I detailed a work crew to start cleaning up the junk that had been allowed to pile up near the entrance to Samoa. Frankly, when I arrived, the town was the biggest mess I ever saw in my life. It seemed liked every house was in need of a paint job at best, or demolition at worst. I looked at the budget and saw that it allowed only $10,000 for continuing maintenance of the nearly 200 houses that Georgia-Pacific owned and rented to employees. In other words, I could spend about $50 per house on upkeep and repairs. I immediately decided to ignore that part of the budget, and instead spent nearly $500,000 sprucing up houses and other community buildings during my first year in Samoa. I was convinced that improving the quality of life of our employees would also increase their loyalty, motivation, and the quality of their work.

Just as I had hoped, my upgrade idea caught on. As eyesores were removed and homes improved, the residents of Samoa began to take pride again in their community. I began a community contest with prizes awarded for the best looking house and the best looking garden, and the competition was fierce. To keep the momentum going, I started a Georgia-Pacific Job Corps, offering any boy aged 16 and 17 in a Georgia-Pacific family living in Samoa or Crandall (another company town twelve miles north of Samoa) a summer job at the then minimum wage of $1.60 an hour. I reasoned that not only would this ensure the completion of numerous community painting and beautification projects, it would also give many boys their first job, and teach a lesson or two about taking pride in your work. I didn't think anyone could disagree with those objectives. I was wrong. The president of the local timberworkers union quickly informed me that he would oppose this program unless the boys were paid union wages. His suggestion would have made the program prohibitively expensive to the company. I called my assistant in to my office, and instructed her to call the owner of the local newspaper. "What are you doing?" the union leader asked me. I said that I wanted to explain to the newspaperman that the union president had killed an opportunity for area teen-agers to obtain a summer job. He quickly weighed what such a story would do to his reputation and support—especially among parents of teen-agers, a number of whom had written me to thank them for the positive difference the summer job was making in their child—and he had an immediate change of heart.

The actions I took during my first year in Samoa seemed to work. The goal Mr. Pamplin had set for me was to turn a $500,000 profit at the Samoa division. When the year ended, I was delighted to report that we had turned a profit of $18 million. My team's performance earned me a beautiful silver bowl and the title of "Georgia-Pacific Man of the Year." It also earned me a few jealous glances from others in the corporate hierarchy who were suspicious of this young new "whippersnapper."

It didn't take me long to take pride in the fact that I worked for Bob Pamplin. He was and is a remarkable man, someone who truly is without parallel in the forest industry. As a manager, I could not have asked for a better mentor. Bob accepted the simple fact that you can not run a profitable large corporation by democratic means. The buck stopped at his desk, and all of the operational policies at Georgia-Pacific were established for the company as a whole from the top. However, implementation of these policies was decentralized to managers at operational locations. G-P's policies were uncomplicated statements of what was expected of the company and from its employees, and provided a discipline that included a work ethic and standards of behavior. Policy goals were stated simply enough that employees knew exactly what was expected of them. Individuals were given responsibility for a job and held responsible for completing it within company policy. Since no two people operate alike, managers were allowed to use their own operational methods within the constraint of company policy. I found this approach to be very conducive to my management style, as I long believed that giving managers what they needed to do their job and letting them do it was the best way to ensure success.

Pamplin was notorious for hating committees, but there was one—and only one—that he allowed to operate at G-P. The Operating Policy Committee was composed of key executives and met four times a year to review the results of the previous quarter and to discuss the next quarter. The committee did not have the power to make decisions. The OPC's purpose was simply to discuss targets and results, and to give every manager a good overview of the company's activities.

Each operating manager set his own goals by preparing annual standards prior to each operating year. The manager submitted a projected profit and loss statement for the coming year. Pamplin personally reviewed these statements with each operating manager. If the goals were unsatisfactory—which meant they did not meet his expectations of doubling sales and profits every five years—a cooperative effort was made to come to agreement. If the manager believed he was incapable of achieving the desired results, then Pamplin's policy was to quickly remove the manager from his position. This was a move he rarely had to make, as he chose managers carefully and wisely. In short, watching Bob Pamplin at work taught me much more than I could ever have learned from a MBA program. Time and again during my years at the helm of Louisiana-Pacific, I would find myself calling upon the lessons and management principles I learned from this unique and visionary leader.

During my first year with G-P, I traveled to Maui to participate in a meeting of the Western Wood Products Association. Also attending the meeting was George Schmidbauer, general manager of F. M. Crawford Lumber Company in Ukiah, California, which was the 19th largest timber company in the United States. George and I had known each other for years, and decided to have dinner together one evening in Maui. We spoke of Frank Crawford, who had founded the company, and his wife, Vivian; both of whom had been killed a year earlier in a tragic plane crash. Schmidbauer was married to Peggy Crawford, Frank and Vivian's daughter, and he told me how Peggy and her two siblings were struggling to keep the company together in the aftermath of their parents death. He wondered aloud if the best course just might be to sell the company. I could never have guessed that this conversation would be the first step on a road full of twists and turns that would eventually lead to the creation of Louisiana-Pacific.

I thought a lot about our conversation after returning to the mainland. The Crawford Lumber Company owned some of the best and most productive timberland and mills in California, as well as some of the most talented people. The more I thought about it, the more I concluded that those timberlands and mills and people would be a great addition to Georgia-Pacific. I was dreaming big, and unlike my experience at Rounds and Kilpatrick, I was confident that in Bob Pamplin, I had a boss who wanted to make those dreams a reality. I called Bud Crofoot, a friend and industry associate, who had also been close to Frank Crawford. I told him that I thought G-P might be interested in buying Crawford Lumber Company, and asked for his opinion. Ironically, just a day or two before our conversation, Bud had told George and Peggy Schmidbauer that Frank had once confided to him on a fishing trip that when the right time came, he was going to sell his company to Georgia-Pacific, as they were the only outfit he regarded as big enough and professional enough to buy him out. It wasn't long before George and I were meeting again, and a few months later the deal was struck. Within an hour or so after the announcement of our agreement was made, the Federal Trade Commission office in San Francisco received an anonymous call from an individual who said that Georgia-Pacific was about to make a purchase of a company that would allow it to secure a monopoly in the lumber market. As was their routine, the FTC opened a file on the complaint. It would be quite some time before I or anyone at G-P would learn about the existence of this file—a file that would play a role in the eventual creation of Louisiana-Pacific.

I enjoyed my job immensely, and enjoyed working with people who dreamed big dreams. In Mid-August of 1969, Mr. Pamplin named me vice president for western operations, a job that required me to relocate to Portland. I was excited about the new opportunity, but melancholy about leaving California. Even though I was moving, I couldn't bring myself to sell my ranch in the hills above Cloverdale. Over the years, I had purchased adjacent lots, and the ranch had grown to over 4,000 acres, and includes one of the largest private lakes in Northern California. Many of those acres are now used to grow some of the best wine grapes in the world, which find their way into some of the best wines in the world—wines that are bottled by Lago di Merlo, ("Lake of Merlo") which is presided over by my son, Harry, Jr, who graduated from California State University in Fresno with a degree in Viticulture. (Check us out at www.lagodimerlo.com)

Though my job came with an office in the executive suite located on the top floor of corporate headquarters, others in the company soon learned that if they wanted to find me, they shouldn't bother looking in my office. The G-P executive suite was something like a very quiet and very elegant southern gentleman's club, where everyone had lunch together in the corporate dining room. I guess it was nice if you liked that sort of thing. It wasn't for me, however. I have always been happier moving rather than sitting, and I preferred to be downstairs, meeting with the people on the operating floors of my division. Better yet, I liked to hit the road, visiting our mills and timberlands, and seeing for myself which mills were operating at maximum efficiency and which timberlands were producing the best lumber.

I was not the first to learn that too much work and too much travel often put too much pressure on a marriage. Nadine and the children had made the move to Portland with me, and I tried to make up for time spent away from them with vacations and gifts, but that was no way to sustain a partnership. Eventually, Nadine and I were to separate and obtain a divorce. I remain friends with her to this day, and we delight in the achievements of Harry, Jr., and of Andrea, who graduated from the University of Oregon and is a successful architect, and Billy, a respected attorney who received his law degree at Stanford.

My success in arranging the purchase of Crawford Lumber Company was motivation for me to continue looking for acquisitions for Georgia-Pacific, and I was soon spearheading the purchase of additional mills and timberland in Fort Bragg, California, Sand Point, Idaho, and Ketchikan, Alaska. One of my fellow G-P executives— only half in jest—said to Mr. Pamplin that I was buying so many mills, they were sure I would buy the same one twice.

✻ ✻ ✻ ✻

While I was looking for G-P acquisitions in the west, others in the company were doing the same in the south. And when G-P acquired a lumber company in Arkansas, the FTC received another complaint that the company was trying to obtain a monopoly in the southern pine plywood industry. The FTC attorney who had been working without much success to build a case against G-P for an alleged redwood monopoly, saw his efforts get new life with the filing of the second complaint.

From March of 1970, when Bob Pamplin received a subpoena from the FTC, until the day after Christmas, 1972, when a final decision was reached, a countless number of hours and dollars were spent in the legal battle that would ultimately lead to decisions that would have a tremendous impact on my life and career.

I first found out about the lawsuit when I was in Idaho, putting the finishing touches on an agreement to buy a sawmill. I called Mr. Pamplin to tell him of the purchase I was about to make for the company. "Can you get out of it?" he asked. When I assured him that the final agreement was contingent upon G-P board approval, he told of the lawsuit and asked me to return to Oregon so he could discuss the case with his executive team. During that meeting, Bob went over the allegations word by word and page by page. The complaint alleged that through the purchase and acquisition of timberlands and mills in the southeast, G-P now had a monopoly in the Southern pine plywood market. The FTC proposed to remedy the situation by requiring G-P to divest itself of eight softwood plywood plants along with a large amount of timberlands and timber cutting rights, and to forbid G-P from making any acquisitions in the forest products industry for ten years.

Given that G-P owned less than one percent of timberlands in the South and that Weyerhauser and International Paper actually owned more timberland than G-P, Bob was confident that the FTC case had no merit. (A government attorney would admit as much after the case was over when he confessed to me that the reason Georgia-Pacific had been targeted was because we were too aggressive in our expansion efforts.) Merit or not, the case dragged on, dragging with it the vitality and innovation of G-P, as company executives devoted the majority of their time to issues surrounding the lawsuit.

As time went on, it became apparent to me that even though I believed that G-P did not have a monopoly, the FTC was simply not going to give in. My job just wasn't fun anymore, and I again felt the urge to be my own man, and to run my own company. I went to Bob and asked him if he would be interested in selling me 51% of three G-P facilities in the California communities of Ukiah, Cloverdale and Oroville. My plan was to run these facilities and to expand, as well, giving G-P 49% ownership in whatever purchases I made. He seemed intrigued, but said he would rather think about it more fully, and discuss it with me after the lawsuit had reached its conclusion.

The FTC finally finished presenting the government's case before a hearing examiner on July 11, 1972. Bob asked G-P's attorneys for an assessment of where the case stood. They were not optimistic. Their research showed that out of approximately 200 recent cases brought by the FTC, the agency had lost only one. Bob concluded that he was in a fight he could not win. He also concluded that he just might be able to win by losing if he could convince the FTC to accept a different remedy than total divestiture of its valuable southern plywood operations. He outlined a proposal to spin out about 20% of G-P's assets into a new company, and to distribute the stock in this new company to G-P stockholders. Bob envisioned that all of the west coast operations that had been under my oversight would be part of the new company, as well as a number of plywood plants and other timber facilities in Texas and Louisiana. The bulk of southern plywood operations would remain with G-P. Bob believed that this proposal would protect the G-P employees who were to become part of the new company by ensuring that they were working for a company that was sound from an operating viewpoint and that had a good chance of continued success. FTC attorneys conducted an initial review of the proposal and said that a settlement seemed to be in reach.

Bob called me to this office, told me of his proposal to the FTC, and wanted to know if I would be willing to serve as President and Chief Executive Officer of the new company. I accepted his offer nearly before the words got out of his mouth. Suddenly, my long-held dream of running my own show was becoming a reality. And the "show" I was to run wasn't just a second-string operation. I added up the assets included in Bob's proposal and determined that the new company would own over 500,000 acres of timberland in the south and on the west coast, and would include seven sawmills and one planing mill in Washington, Oregon and Idaho; six plants in Ohio, twelve plants in Texas and Louisiana, and a 50% interest in a pulp mill and sawmill in Ketchikan, Alaska. In sum, the spin-off would begin operations with $327 million in assets, 6,000 employees, and 46 plants and mills. On day one, it would be the largest lumber company in America.

The question of what to name the new company was decided when Harry Kane, the Chief Financial Officer of G-P, said that since the idea of combining a southern state with the Pacific Ocean had worked so well for Georgia-Pacific, the spin-off should be called "Texas-Pacific." A day or two later he reported back that there already was a railroad operating under that name, so a decision was made to call the new company "Louisiana-Pacific."

12-27-72

Average: +.98
Volume: 18,440,000

Louisiana-Pacific Stock

O	H	L	C	V
25	30⅞	25	30¾	28,900

Previous Day's Close		Open	High	Low	Close	Volume
ON 41⅞		41⅞	44	41½	43⅜	51,200

2-27-72 Bond Market

4% 1994	101		101	101	101	75
4% 1996	87½		87¾	86¼	87¾	283

*   *   *   *   *   *   *   *   *

PLYWOOD FUTURES

CURRENT 1/2" EXTERIOR CD PRICE $128.80 which is equivalent to a commodity price of $116.50 .

CHICAGO BOARD OF TRADE PLYWOOD

	Previous Day Close	Contract Vol. (Carloads)	Open	High	Low	Close
January	167^{50}	74	169	173	168^{50}	$172^{20\text{-}80}$
February						
March	153	135	155	160	154^{00}	157^{80}
April	148	55	149^{50}	152^{50}	149^{50}	151
May	141^{60}	331	144	144^{60}	143	144^{60}
August						
September	136	322	138	139^{50}	138	139^{50}
October						
November	131	25	134	135	134	135
December						
TOTAL	942					

One of the most exciting days of my life was when L-P stock began trading on the New York Stock Exchange.

On December 18, 1972, the Federal Trade Commission convened in Washington, D.C. for a final hearing on the proposed spin-off. My testimony before the Commission was to be my my first public appearance as President of Louisiana-Pacific, and I had given a great deal of thought to my remarks. I wanted the Commission, L-P employees, and L-P stockholders to know that I was at the helm of a profitable, growing company that would be a good corporate citizen and a worthy competitor of Georgia-Pacific. Eight days later, the Commission granted its final approval and on December 27, 1972 the symbol "LPX" began trading on the New York Stock Exchange.

ᚹᚹᚹᚹ

CHAPTER 9

Merlo's Maxims on Leadership

IT IS A LONG WAY FROM the poverty of my childhood home in the lumber yard to the executive suite of Louisiana-Pacific, and as a young man I never could have imagined where my life's journey would lead. Serving as CEO of a major American corporation is a job rich in both challenges and rewards. It is a job where every decision you make impacts the life and future of thousands of employees, and where each of those decisions is open for second-guessing by those employees, your stockholders, and the media. It is a job of incredible highs and humbling lows. It is a job I loved for over twenty years.

Detailing a chronological history of my years at Louisiana-Pacific is not why I wrote this book, and is something I will leave to others. Frankly, I doubt that many would be interested in a rehashing of profit and loss statements, sales numbers, and acquisitions. What I hope you are interested in, however, are the philosophies and values that guided me during my more than two decades at the helm of L-P—philosophies and values that I believe can be used by all those who aspire to leadership.

In fact, the more I reflect, the more it becomes clear to me that whatever successes and accomplishments I achieved at Georgia-Pacific and L-P were the direct result of the lessons I learned as a young boy—most of them instilled in me by Mama. So if you took my advice and poured yourself a glass of wine when you began this book, you have my permission to pour yourself another, while I share "Merlo's Maxims."

Surround yourself with good people and remember that success is being part of a team

The first management decisions I made at Louisiana-Pacific were in selecting the members of my executive team. I had an agreement with Mr. Pamplin to not raid Georgia-Pacific by taking all his "number one" people. Truth be told, that suited me fine, as it was the "number two" people who were usually doing all the work that their bosses got credit for. It was these folks who were lean and hungry and hankering for an opportunity to be part of a team. Many of them would come with me and stay with L-P for the remainder of their careers.

If there was one lesson Mama instilled in my siblings and me it was the importance of teamwork. Mama was the leader of our team, but everyone had a job to do—be it cleaning the chicken coop, washing the dishes or mopping the floor—and everyone was responsible for getting the job done right and not letting the team down. There was no tolerance for excuses, and if you tried to blame your failure on someone else you would be rewarded with Mama's most withering glare.

I kept all this in mind as I put together my management team. As compared to other corporations, where there seemed to be an endless supply of vice-presidents, (and an endless supply of buck-passing) L-P's executive suite was small. I think I am safe in saying that we were the only company in American who reached over three billion dollars in sales with only two vice-presidents. And you know what? Having twenty vice-presidents wouldn't have helped us reach three billion in sales one minute sooner. (In fact, it probably would have delayed us from reaching that plateau.) I once heard an executive from another successful forest products company advise his employees to always remember that they worked for a billion dollar company and to act accordingly. I advised my team something different—I advised them to always remember how we got there.

If you didn't know better, you might think that helping Mama around the house was hard work. I know that cleaning, sweeping, and picking vegetables doesn't sound like much fun—especially if you are a kid—but the truth is that Mama made being part of her "team" a whole lot of fun. If we grumbled or groaned about a chore she assigned to us, she would simply remind us to "Make work fun." It didn't take long for my brothers and I to figure out some contest to see who would be the best—and the fastest—at completing the chore.

When I had the opportunity to lead my "team", I remembered Mama's advice. I expected L-P's employees to work hard and to give their best—but I also encouraged them to enjoy themselves. Birthdays were to be remembered, corporate successes were to be celebrated, and company outings to sporting events were to be enjoyed.

Given that the importance of team and having fun were two lessons Mama instilled to me as a boy, perhaps it was natural that I have had a lifelong interest in sports and athletics. I have written about my participation in track and field during my high school years, my involvement in boxing tournaments during my time in the military, and the tradition of timber companies sponsoring softball teams. Keeping in shape was important to me and helped me to better do my job. I knew it would help our employees do their job better, as well, so from the very beginning at L-P, I encouraged physical fitness through sponsorship of recreational teams for employees, and through weight-loss incentive programs. I became friendswith the remarkable physical fitness guru Jack LaLanne, and our company magazine included Jack's tips for physical fitness.

Flanked by two remarkable women—Pam Selis, who served as L-P's Director of Corporate Communications before her untimely death, and Jeana Yeager, who, along with Dick Rutan,in 1986, flew the first ever around the world nonstop un-refueled flight.

I played many sports in my youth, but tennis certainly wasn't one of them. Back then, it still had a reputation of being a "rich man's" sport, and you also would have been hard pressed to find more than a handful of tennis players in the rough and tumble timber industry. This helps to explain why I was more than a bit skeptical when my assistant, Flo Newton, brought a young tennis professional named Brian Parrott into my office in the fall of 1977.

Brian was there to ask for my support of a professional tennis tournament, and the more he talked, the more impressed I was. He knew the tennis business like I knew the lumber business. His love of and enthusiasm for tennis was contagious. Brian was the guiding force behind the "Pacific Coast Indoor," which was an annual professional tennis tournament played in Portland. Tennis had been experiencing an increase in popularity, and the prize money offered at professional tournaments was increasing. Brian wanted to attract top name players to Portland and he needed an infusion of cash to do it. He proposed that L-P donate $7,500 to a tournament, which would be re-named "The Louisiana-Pacific Invitational."

While $7,500 may not sound like much to a corporation the size of Louisiana-Pacific, it was a lot of money to someone who grew up in poverty. I also knew that L-P did not belong to Harry Merlo. It belonged to our tens of thousands of stockholders, and if I was to agree with Brian's proposal, then I had to conclude that the investment would pay dividends for the company. Even though L-P had been on its own for four years, there were still those who regarded us as nothing more than a step-child of Georgia-Pacific. I concluded that a tennis tournament bearing L-P's name would send a message that we were a separate company with a separate identity, and I told Brian we were on board. I still shake my head at the fact that my decision to support this tournament would start me down a path that would, for a time, make me one of the most talked about figures in the world of tennis.

The first "L-P Invitational" was a success, and at Brian's request, I opened my home so that three of the participants could stay there during the tournament. Dennis Ralston, Erik vanDillen and Tom Gorman were three prominent professionals of the time, and I was very much impressed with their athleticism and their attitude. Over the next few years, L-P would increase our support of the tournament to $50,000 and the level of players traveling to Portland would increase correspondingly. Soon, elite players like Stan Smith, Ile Nastase, Guillermo Vilas, and Boris Becker were making their way to Portland.

In 1981, Brian again came to my office with a proposal. The Davis Cup—the prestigious annual international tennis competition where the best of the best play not as an individual, but as a representative of their country—was looking for an American city to host the semi-final match between the United States and Australia. Brian believed that Portland would be the perfect venue, and he needed L-P's financial backing to make it happen. The Davis Cup would be covered by media from around the world, and I again saw it as an opportunity to increase the awareness of Louisiana-Pacific, and to show off our home city. I committed $175,000 to the effort, and was delighted when Portland beat out Boston for the right to host the semi-final in October 1981.

The three days that encompassed the Davis Cup competition were some of the most memorable and enjoyable of my life. Portlanders embraced the competition, and the 36,000 available tickets were sold out in just nine days, ensuring that the Davis Cup would have the largest paid attendance in its history. A series of gala parties and receptions, including one I was proud to host in my home, put out the red carpet for officials from the Unite States Tennis Association, our visitors from Australia and for a large delegation of visitors from Japan who were representing Nippon Electric Company, the giant electronics conglomerate that was the major sponsor of the worldwide Davis Cup competition. The tennis was also first rate, as the American team of John McEnroe, Roscoe Tanner and Peter Fleming delighted the fans with an American victory.

1984 Davis Cup Team Clockwise, Coach Arthur Ashe, Jimmy Arias, Jimmy Connors, Peter Fleming, Aaron Krickstein, John McEnroe

The competition was the first time I had the opportunity to meet McEnroe, who arrived in Portland with a reputation as a fiery competitor with a tendency to lose his temper on the court when a call did not go his way. McEnroe managed to be on his best behavior in Portland, but as I would learn later, his good manners were to be the exception and not the rule. I was greatly impressed by the captain of the American team, tennis great Arthur Ashe, who exuded class and integrity.

I have been delighted to open my Portland home for a number of charitable and philanthropic galas, but the celebration dinner I hosted for the Davis Cup was the most enjoyable and memorable of all. A large tent was set up on my lawn, and 250 guests joined Arthur Ashe, John McEnroe, Jimmy Connors, all the Davis Cup participants, and much of the "royalty" of the tennis world for a perfect evening of great food, good will, and international camaraderie. The entertainment was provided by a wonderful Portlander named Bruce Kelly and his choral group, "The New Oregon Singers," who had performed around the world for many years. Bruce also served as master of ceremonies and had the audience roaring with his good natured kidding of the

Boris Becker was an unknown 19 year old when he burst upon the scene by winning the 1985 L-P Tennis Invitational. Six months later he would win Wimbledon.

participants and his inability to understand the thick accent of the Australian team captain, Neal Fraser. I still laugh when I recall the Japanese Chairman of NEC rising to speak, and apologizing to all those present for his poor English. "No need to apologize," deadpanned Bruce, "I can understand you a lot better than the Australian."

My decision to involve L-P with the Davis Cup competition also paid great dividends for the City of Portland and all of Oregon. At the conclusion of their stay here, the chief executive officer of NEC revealed that they were on the verge of locating a new manufacturing facility in the United States. They had previously narrowed their search to two American cities—but because of what they saw and experienced in Portland, they were now expanding that list to three cities. Indeed, NEC eventually decided to build their new 200 acre facility in the Portland suburb of Hillsboro. In a letter to Frank Ivancie, the then Mayor of Portland, Shozo Shimuzu, Senior Vice President of NEC, wrote, "Our impression of the city and Oregon at the time of the tournament had a bearing on our decision to locate in Oregon." It was a decision that would eventually lead to some eight hundred new jobs, one hundred million dollars in economic development, and would help attract other electronic and high-tech companies to what has now become known as Oregon's "Silicon Forest." Not a bad return on a $175,000 investment!

Following the success of the Davis Cup matches in Portland, I watched with interest as the competition moved on to Cincinnati and St. Louis. Corporations in those cities served as the sponsor of the matches, but ticket sales were far below what we achieved in Portland. So in 1984, our offer to make L-P the presenting sponsor for all Davis Cup matches hosted in the United States was quickly accepted. Brian and I chose Atlanta from a list of eleven American cities bidding to host the quarterfinal match between the United States and Argentina. Thanks to our staging team, which was led by Brian and tennis professional Tom Gorman, the competition was back on firm ground, with a record paid attendance of 48,000 over the three days of competition. Arthur Ashe was still the captain of the American team, which consisted of John McEnroe, Peter Fleming and the one and only Jimmy Connors. After a win in Atlanta, the American team returned to Portland, where sell-out crowds cheered them on to a semi-final victory over Australia.

The finals of the 1984 Davis Cup were to be held in Sweden, and I was excited to represent L-P in Stockholm. My excitement was to turn to embarrassment as I watched first Connors and then McEnroe in their matches. I wasn't embarrassed by their tennis skills, which were remarkable. I was, however, embarrassed by their behavior. Both shouted vulgarities at the umpire when they disagreed with line calls, and McEnroe generally acted like an ill-behaved three-year old, pouting, stomping on flowers that had been placed near the court, and throwing whatever he could find, including small fishing nets the young ball boys and girls used to retrieve tennis balls. I had no doubt that had Mama been in the audience, she would have grabbed Connors and McEnroe by the ears and taught them a thing or two about manners.

As the CEO of the sponsor of the American team, I was embarrassed beyond words. What's more, I knew that L-P stockholders, who, after all, are the ones who put up the money to sponsor our team, would share my embarrassment. Upon my return to Portland, I convened a meeting with Brian and my team of L-P executives to consider our options, including complete withdrawal from our contract with the United States Tennis Association. I decided not to take that course of action because of my admiration for Arthur Ashe. I knew that Arthur, a true gentleman, shared my embarrassment of the behavior of our team, and I thought that our withdrawal would not reflect well on his leadership.

Therefore, I decided to issue a call for a "Code of Conduct," stating that if the United States Tennis Association was interested in retaining the monetary support of L-P, then they must require that all members of the United States Davis Cup team sign a statement acknowledging that they represent all citizens of the United States, and that they agree to treat with respect those individuals they come into contact with as a member of the American team.

I put this proposal in a letter, and sent it to the United States Tennis Association with copies also mailed to Arthur, the American team, and our friends at NEC. So the 51,000 shareholders of L-P would know my position, I also released the letter to the media on December 30, 1984. It read as follows:

> *"Throughout 1984, Louisiana-Pacific has been proud to sponsor America's pursuit of the Davis Cup—proud, that is, until Sweden.*
>
> *We believe America's team must always set a positive example for young players around the world.*
>
> *True, our team clearly shines if one were to consider only the skills of the game. But we fail badly when it comes to living up to minimum behavior for standards on the court, during awards ceremonies and at other official Davis Cup events.*
>
> *Common courtesy demands civil behavior from U.S. team members. Abusive language, gestures, abuse of rackets, balls and courtside accessories—all such irresponsible and immature*

*behavior should not be tolerated. Respect for our opponents'
anthems and flags is basic. Discipline must be enforced.*

*Louisiana-Pacific has no quarrel with an individual's
right to be himself, yet we strongly believe team members—who
willingly represent this country—must recognize that personal
preferences give way to the greater responsibility of the flag and
the good of the game.*

*We also must recognize our responsibility to L-P
shareholders, whose money we are investing in sponsoring the
U.S. Davis Cup team. They watch television and read about
the success or shortcomings of "America's best," too.*

*In a spirit of fairness and with the best interests of the
sport in mind, Louisiana-Pacific...respectfully suggests a
players' code of conduct be immediately adopted by the USTA
for Davis Cup competition.*

*Unless we are assured you have the authority to effect such
constructive changes, we will move to withdraw our sponsorship
and support of the U.S. Davis Cup team."*

I expected the letter might make a splash or two in the tennis
world, but I was surprised that by Near Year's Day, the letter was
reported in most of the world's major newspapers, leading to a
worldwide reaction—a reaction that could be summed up in one
word: "Amen."

First came the editorials from major newspapers unaccustomed
to commenting about tennis, such as the New York Times and the
London Times. My hometown paper, The Oregonian, editorialized
that "Harry Merlo has served an ace." Then came the letters and phone
calls—thousands of letters and phone calls. They came from business

leaders, educators, tennis fans, L-P shareholders and average citizens. It seemed like the only person who took offense to my letter was—you guessed it—John McEnroe. He called me a "jerk" and criticized me for "grandstanding." Arthur Ashe proved again what a class act he was by sending me a letter in which he assumed responsibility for McEnroe and Connors' boorish behavior. I still have the original of that letter, and share a part of it here for the first time.

Dear Harry:

…Your continuing support of our United States Davis Cup effort is appreciated. Although some of the members of the team were upset that they read about your letter before receiving it in the mail, the sentiments you expressed were certainly felt by a wide range of people and had diverse support. As you are probably aware, we have already moved to make major corrections which will redress some of your complaints.

You know, a great deal of the fault—if it can be termed as such—is mine alone. I knew full well a year ago the down side of trying to pull together Jimmy Connors and John McEnroe on the same team at the same time. While some people, including quite a few in the USTA, thought I had pulled a coup, other said "it will never work." In the end, the egos were just too strong and years of self-centered lifestyles took precedence over a wholesome image. Some of our top players have been allowed to get away with so many things for so long that no one is going to change those habits.

Sincerely, Arthur R. Ashe, Jr.

★★★★

Eventually, the United States Tennis Association did adopt a version of my proposed code of conduct, making it clear the standards of behavior that were expected by tennis professionals representing the United States. L-P continued its support of the Portland tournament for a number of years, but over time I began to look for other sporting events which would be a wise expenditure of funds. My involvement with tennis did infuse me with a passion for the game. I have a court at my house and like to play with friends, including Brian Parrott. Give me a call sometime if you want to play!

The L-P sponsorship of tennis established us as a company that promoted healthy activities, and that cared about our community. We were a company that was willing to make a difference, and an opportunity to do just that presented itself on the unlikely venue of a soccer field. In the 1970's Portland was one of a number of cities that experienced a boom in the interest in soccer, and the city was home to the Portland Timbers, a franchise in the new North American Soccer League. After initial success, the franchise soon found itself in financial trouble. I was actually not a big fan of soccer, but keeping the team here was a matter of civic pride. I arranged for L-P to buy the Timbers for $500,000, and I pledged the net income of the team to six community service and cultural organizations, Portland United Way, Portland Opera Association, Portland Junior Symphony, The Oregon Museum of Science and Industry, and the Oregon Youth Soccer Association. I believed this arrangement would encourage people to attend because ticket sales would also benefit their favorite charity or cultural activity. As part of the purchase, I also insisted on a stipulation that players under contract would have off-season community service as a condition of employment, making player talents available to schools and youth soccer organizations for clinics, thereby promoting the growth of the sport. And how the sport has grown! While a professional soccer league still struggles to survive, youth soccer games dominate the weekend schedules of millions of parents and the term "soccer mom" is now part of our national vocabulary.

While L-P's involvement with professional soccer lasted only three years, it did lead to a friendship with Clive Charles, one of the most courageous and remarkable individuals I have ever met. Born in Britain, Charles has spent his adult life playing soccer in Europe and the United States. He was playing for the Portland Timbers when we first crossed paths, and I was impressed by his enthusiasm and the joy with which he played. I was still impressed years later when Clive, now retired from playing, returned to Portland to begin his coaching career. Clive's first coaching job was with a local high school, but he truly found his niche as the coach of both the men and women's team at the University of Portland, an outstanding Catholic university. I had long been an admirer and supporter of the University, and was sympathetic when Clive came to me to sketch out his dreams of making the University a soccer powerhouse, and the need to upgrade the soccer facilities. I made a large donation, and was honored when the University chose to name the new soccer venue "Merlo Field."

I spent many an hour at the side of Merlo Field watching as Clive became the greatest coach in more than a century of University of Portland athletics, leading his men's and women's teams to 439 victories, 20 national playoff berths, 13 league titles, and a NCAA national women's championships in 2002. Clive also coached the United State's men's national soccer team to a bronze medal in the 1999 Pan American Games and a fourth place finish in the 2000 Olympic Games. To watch Clive coach was to watch a man who truly loved his job and who truly made a positive difference for all the members of his teams. He demanded the best from his teams, and he got it. He taught more than soccer skills—he also instilled in his team members the same values that Mama instilled in her children—honesty, integrity, and persistence. Clive waged a courageous battle against prostate cancer through much of 2003, but it was to be a battle that he could not win. He passed away on August 26, 2003 at the far-too-young age of 51. I visited Clive frequently during the final months and weeks of his life, and will never forget the last time I saw him—only hours before he fell into a coma. Clive looked up at me from his bed, and whispered, "Harry, we gave it a hell of a go." So we did, my friend. So we did.

Clive Charles, an extraordinary soccer coach and an even more extraordinary person with assistant coach Bill Irwin.

Merlo Field under the lights, University of Portland.

My friend Earle Chiles joins me at Merlo Field as the University of Portland Pilots celebrate winning the 2002 NCAA women's soccer championship.

It's hard to lead from behind a desk

When Mama put together one of her famous meals she insisted on personally inspecting and selecting the ingredients. She would go into the garden to pick the ripest tomato, or into the chicken coop to point out the plumpest chicken. In short, she wanted to see, smell and size up the ingredients she needed to succeed. I was the same way as CEO. The way I looked at it, I wasn't leading or learning if I was sitting behind my desk. Listening to a phone report on how a new mill was operating could not compare to actually seeing the mill for myself.

So, for my twenty-two years as CEO, I was constantly on the fly—literally. Thanks to one of the most advanced aviation departments in corporate America, I was able to hop in a jet and personally visit our operations and talk with as many members of the L-P team as I could—my personal record was visiting seven L-P plants in one very long and tiring day!

I applied the same standard to L-P's board of directors. Most corporate boards hold their quarterly meetings in company headquarters or perhaps at a luxury resort. I insisted that our board meetings be held in the cities that were home to one of the 112 L-P plants, and that part of the agenda included an on-site tour. My goal was to have board members who weren't just rubber stamps—but who knew the ins and outs of all L-P's operations. When Ralph Voss, former vice-president of First Interstate Bank, and one of L-P's outstanding board members, retired from the board in 1985, he delivered remarks where he listed all the cities he had traveled to as a board member, and he offered this observation: "With all of this, I cannot claim to know all there is to know about L-P and its operations, but Harry has done his damndest to let me know all there is to know." It was music to my ears.

One final point on our aviation department is worth mentioning: While I have no doubt that the department paid for itself in the ability it gave my management team and me to personally visit all our operations, I also devised a more concrete way for it to pay for itself. After a few years of operation, our aviation department had gained such a reputation for excellence, that it was recognized by a business aviation magazine as the best corporate aviation department in America. As a result, other corporations, businesses, and even professional sports teams began to inquire about leasing our planes and pilots. Getting the complete certification that would allow this

PROFESSIONAL PILOT

DECEMBER 1982

Flight Department of the Year
Louisiana-Pacific

Av Director Montel Work (left),
Chairman Harry Merlo (center) and
Chief Pilot David Dix (right) pose with
department members at HIO, home base
for two Learjet 25s and Gulfstream 2.

Charter Profiles

As CEO, I was the one who stood in front, but it was the work of all those behind me that won L-P the "flight department of the year" award from Professional Pilot Magazine.

✦✦✦✦

was a complex task that the FAA estimated would take six months. We finished it in three. The credit for the success of the L-P aviation department goes to the remarkable Flo Newton. Her leadership made our aviation department the best in the business, just as she now makes Global Aviation of Hillsboro, Oregon, one of the best air charter operations anywhere.

If you never share a dollar, you will never share a million

I have never forgotten the credo that Mama shared each time she sent a money order to Boy's Town. When I became CEO of Louisiana-Pacific I made Mama's philosophy the company philosophy, as well. Indeed, L-P's record of community generosity and corporate philanthropy during my years at the helm is probably the accomplishment in which I take the most pride.

My philosophy was simple. L-P's 12,000 employees lived in the hundreds of communities that were home to our facilities. It was in the best interests of our employees and their families that their communities would have good schools, parks, museums, and social service organizations. Therefore, it was in the best interests of L-P to generously donate to those causes. And donate we did, to countless non-profit and philanthropic organizations, especially those that focused on opening doors for young people.

One of the organizations that impressed me the most was Northwest Medical Teams. Headquartered in Portland, (and now called Medical Teams International) this remarkable humanitarian organization made a difference in the poorest corners of the world. I especially recall the day when I received a briefing from the Northwest Medical Team staff about a project they were proposing in the slums of Mexico City, Mexico. They showed me photographs of the largest garbage dump I had ever seen. My heart nearly broke when they explained that hundreds of poverty-stricken children were using the dump as both a playground and a place to scavenge for food. The dream of Northwest Medical Teams was to pave over that dump and to build a beautiful new school on the site. I could almost hear Mama whisper "If you never give a dollar, you will never give a million." It didn't take me long to decide that L-P would generously donate to the cause, and was delighted when the project was completed and I received reports of the difference the school was making in the lives of the neighborhood's children.

I also encouraged employees to donate their time to the cause of their choice, and tried to set an example through my involvement with

Thanks to Medical Teams International, the Las Aguilas School was built on what was once a garbage dump.

organizations like the Salvation Army, Special Olympics, the American Red Cross, American Acadamy of Achievment, Goodwill Industries, Habitat for Humanity, Hugh O'Brian Youth Foundation, Junior

Achievement, Loaves and Fishes, New Avenues for Youth, the Oregon Food Bank, Court Appointed Special Advocates, the American Heart Association, the Anti-Defamation League, Boys and Girls Clubs, the Oregon Museum of Science and Industry, Boys' Towns of Italy, Inc. and many others.

Along with money and time, L-P also donated land. Drive 32 miles north of Eureka, California on Highway 101 and you will find the Harry Merlo State Recreation Area—a beautiful 830 acre park bordering on a lagoon that is a popular place for families who like to fish and explore the ocean

Boys Town of Italy, Inc. is proud to present the Humanitarian Award to Harry Merlo on May 13, 1985.

beaches. This and other donations of land would lead in 1987 to L-P proudly receiving a merit award from the California Parks and Recreation Department.

Of all the philanthropic projects and causes that L-P supported and that I have supported personally, the one that means the most to me is one that is located where I was born and raised. Indeed, one of the proudest days of my life occurred on August 29, 1987—25 years and two weeks after Mama's death—when I returned to Stirling City to dedicate the Clotilde Merlo Park. The story of how this park came to be is one that I delight in sharing.

In 1983, Diamond International—the company that had evolved from the Diamond Match Company—was up for sale. As CEO of

Louisiana Pacific, I was anxious to bid on the company's assets, as I believed they would be a valuable addition to the company. Since the assets included the land once occupied by the old Stirling City mill site, which had fallen into disrepair after the mill was shut down in 1958, there were probably emotional reasons behind my interest, as well. Eventually, I bid $850 million for the company and its assets, but lost out to the $900 million bid of Sir James Goldsmith, the legendary British business tycoon who had become a major player in the forest products industry with his purchase of Crown Zellerbach. Goldsmith then contacted me and said he was interested in selling some of the assets he had just purchased. In the process of negotiating an agreement, we became close friends, and Sir James, who had been knighted by Queen Elizabeth II in 1976, insisted that I call him "Jimmy."

Eventually, I told Jimmy of my childhood in Stirling City, and confessed that I had long harbored the dream of buying the land where Dago Town once sat, and turning it into a park to honor Mama and the immigrant pioneers who had helped to build the mill. I explained that there was an annual "Old Timers" picnic for retired employees of what was Diamond Match Company, and that every summer the picnic was held in a dry, grassy, treeless field in Chico, where the temperature often reached 105 degrees. My dream was to build a beautiful park in Stirling City that they could call their own. I concluded by telling Jimmy that I would pay any amount of money he wanted. He considered my offer and then told me that I couldn't buy it. I was devastated and asked him why. He replied, "You can't buy it because I'm going to give it to you." That is precisely what he did. Cancer claimed Jimmy at the age of 64 in 1997. I will always remember his remarkable generosity.

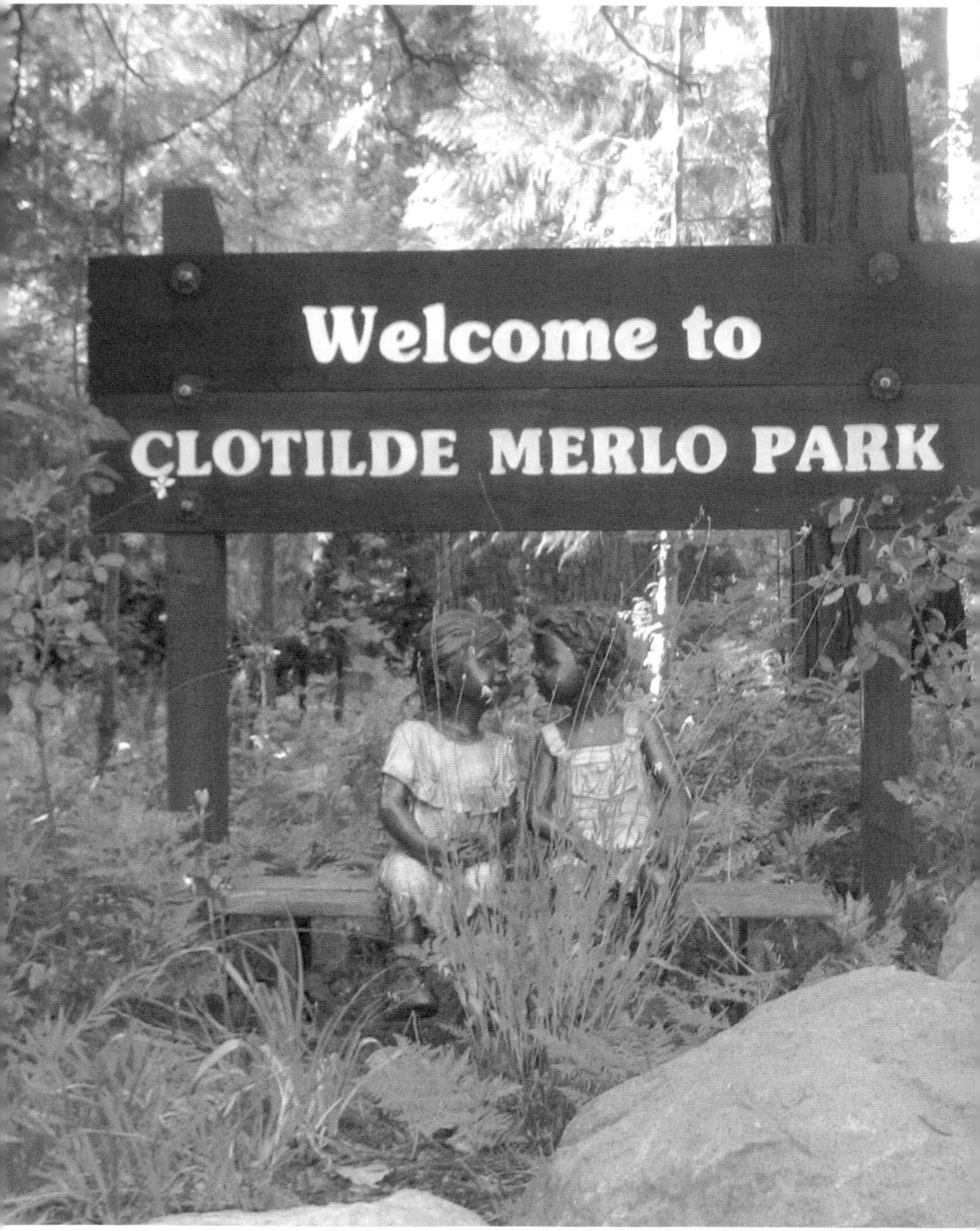
Welcome to
CLOTILDE MERLO PARK

CLOTILDE MERLO PARK
DEDICATED AUGUST 29, 1987

BY HARRY A. MERLO IN MEMORY OF HIS MOTHER WHOSE PERSONAL TRAITS OF COMMON SENSE, COURAGE AND STRENGTH OF PURPOSE REPRESENT THE WORKING PRINCIPLES AND PHILOSOPHY OF HER SON DURING HIS DISTINGUISHED CAREER.

IT IS THE INTENTION OF THE HARRY A. MERLO FOUNDATION THAT THIS PARK BRING PEACE, TRANQUILITY AND DIGNITY IN REMEMBRANCE OF THE MANY EMIGRANTS WHO, IN THE FIRST DECADES OF THE 1900'S, SETTLED IN THE COMMUNITY OF STIRLING CITY.

Mama loved being close to nature and she so appreciated the beauty of the land. There is no place closer to nature or where the land is more beautiful than in the park named for her. To walk through the thirty acre park is to see majestic trees of all kinds—ponderosa, sugar pine, cedar, white and Douglas fir, black oak, aspen, and manzanita. You will also find four small lakes, a cascading waterfall, and a number of Blacktail deer, grey squirrels and many species of birds.

I also placed in the park a bronze statue of Mama returning from the garden that was created by my friend, famed sculptor Lorenzo Ghiglieri. Lorenzo is also responsible for a beautiful sculpture of Jesus Christ, which is placed in the small wedding chapel that is included in the park. It was in this chapel where many couples—including my son and his wife—have been married.

Heisman Trophy Winner and NFL great Herschel Walker

Actor Hugh O'Brian and former Soviet Union President Mikhail Gorbachev

The park also features a number of bronze statues of children. Look in one direction and you will see a likeness of a child throwing a baseball. Walk down a trail and there is a sculpture of a small child turning a cartwheel. Look another direction and there is a child dropping a fishing line in the lake. These sculptures helped to send a message that as beautiful and special as it is, the park is not the best monument to Mama. Her best legacy is her children. Mama could not give her children money or prestige. But she gave us much more than that— she instilled in us commitments to hard work, honesty, always doing our best, and an unshakable belief in God. These are commitments that have guided my steps throughout my life and career.

Listen to the "small voices"

My background in Dago Town made me especially respectful of the fact that all wisdom does not originate in Washington, D.C. or on Wall Street. I also believed that every stockholder—no matter how few shares they happened to hold—was deserving of respect. On one occasion, I received a letter from a gentleman in Pennsylvania who had recently purchased 100 shares of stock, and was dissatisfied with a management decision. As was the practice, he promptly received a letter of explanation from our stockholders relations department. A copy of the gentleman's letter was on my desk when I returned from a business trip overseas, and I decided to give him a call to personally discuss in detail the reasons behind the decision I had made. He seemed surprised to hear from me, and we had a very productive conversation.

I thought nothing more of it, and was stunned when the well-known financial columnist Louis Rukeyser made the phone conversation a national news story. The disgruntled stockholder had

Mama's optimism and patriotism were the inspiration for L-P's "Yes We Can" campaign. From left to right are John Hart, treasurer and controller; Don Holman, corporate secretary and me, chairman and president.

been so impressed by my phone call that he wrote a letter to Rukeyser, stating "To say I was shocked is putting it mildly. And I have written you just to say the small investor really is being listened to in companies that are serious about their business…And you can pretty well guess where I am putting my money when I purchase more stock."

Rukeyser shared all this in his column, and added his own comment that "If capitalism is to survive in the face of ideological competition and muddled political management, it had better look to its own followers—and to its own failings. And while the company president can't be on the phone all day every day, a little more of the kind of communication related here could win the system a lot more friends."

Optimism—and patriotism—are powerful forces

No matter how strapped we were for cash or how dismal the situation looked, Mama never gave up—and she wouldn't let her children give up, either. Mama was the most optimistic person I have ever known. She knew that with little hard work or a little extra effort, you could overcome the toughest of challenges.

If there was one thing that Mama loved almost as much as her children, it was America. When my brothers and I began to achieve some professional success in the early 1960's, we pooled our resources to send Mama on a trip to Italy. She reunited with relatives, went sight-seeing in Rome, and visited the grave of her first husband. It was an emotional trip to her native land, but it was clear that her heart and her home were in America. In one of the letters she sent me during her trip, she wrote, *"Italy! I'd rather be on Social Security in America than a marchese in Italy. I bought an iron for my niece and her husband wouldn't let her use it because the electricity costs too much. The light bulbs in Italy are so tiny you have to strike a match to find the light."*

Mama's optimism and patriotism were the inspiration for a campaign that I began at LP in the 1970's. It was a time when America was in a funk. High inflation, high unemployment, and high interest rates had sent the economy—and the timber industry—into a tailspin. There seemed to be a growing consensus that our best days were behind us.

I knew that Mama wouldn't stand such pessimism, and I wasn't about to sit still for it either, so I initiated a company wide campaign entitled "Yes We Can!" That simple motto was printed on buttons, bumper stickers, and bulletin boards. I toured our operations across the nation, spreading the word that LP's—and America's—best days were yet to come. And our quarterly company newsletter included essays carrying the same message.

I feel compelled to share part of an essay that ran nearly a quarter century-ago, because the words ring just as true today:

> *Okay America, on your feet. For too long we've been waiting for others to solve our problems. City Hall. The State House. Uncle Sam.*
>
> *And the problems get bigger. Things don't work. We're immobilized by partisanship and petty politics.*
>
> *Worst of all, we're beginning to doubt ourselves. Maybe Yankee Doodle isn't so dandy anymore. There's a gnawing feeling that the good old days may be gone forever.*
>
> *And we wait. And feel helpless. And grow depressed.*
>
> *Well, it's time we stopped fretting about America and started doing something about America. Each one of us. Right where we live. Starting today.*

☆☆☆☆

And that's where you come in. Do something positive in your own neighborhood. Make your home and yard a place to be proud of. Help your neighbor do the same. Lend a hand. Encourage the young. Reach out to the disadvantaged. Take control of things you can control.

A better America depends on better Americans.

Together we can turn things around. YES WE CAN!

Corny? Some might think so. But I think it was right on target, and very effective. The Yes We Can! Campaign succeeded in uniting L-P's thousands of employees across the country in a common belief that their company and their country could persevere through challenging times.

Embrace change (Or how Oriented Strand Board was born)

In many ways, Mama was a very traditional Italian wife and mother. She cooked the meals, cleaned the house, and cared for the children. But in so many other ways, Mama provided an example of how to embrace change. It took courage to set sail for America with a young son and to marry a man she had met only through correspondence. When the Merlo family finances reached a critically low level, it was Mama who became the family breadwinner. And when life with my father became intolerable, it was Mama who moved to Berkeley with my brothers and me and began a new chapter in her life.

Throughout my years at L-P, I tried to be a leader who was not wed to the way things were "always done." Rather, I tried to be a leader who anticipated and accepted change. Indeed, I believe L-P might not have survived the 1970's, had I not embraced change.

Within a few years of assuming the helm at Louisiana-Pacific, I couldn't help but smile at the fact that it was the actions of a government agency—the Federal Trade Commission—that led to the creation of L-P, and it was the actions of a government agency—the Department of Interior—that might well lead to the destruction of L-P.

Environmentalists make most Northwest timbermen see red. Louisiana-Pacific's Harry Merlo sees green.

Friend of the spotted owl

By Marc Beauchamp

Louisiana-Pacific Chairman Harry Merlo
Fighting environmentalists with innovative wood products.

Installing Louisiana-Pacific siding
The product is 25% cheaper than cedar.

L-P's move into oriented strand board led to this Forbes *article, headlined, "Environmentalists make most Northwest timbermen see red. Louisiana-Pacific's Harry Merlo sees green." April 30, 1990.*

With each passing month, it seemed like the federal government was placing more and more timber off limits from harvesting. It dawned on me that if things didn't change, L-P would consist of hard-working employees, world class mills, and absolutely no forest products to keep the employees working and the mills running. I had a feeling that government policies were not going to change, so I knew that L-P would have to change if we were to survive.

All that was weighing on my mind as I attended an annual trade show sponsored by the National Association of Home Builders in 1978. I was walking through the maze of exhibition booths with Jim Eisses, one of my two vice presidents, when we came upon a display that brought me to a halt. It was a booth promoting a building product called "waferwood," which was being advertised as an alternative to the traditional plywood building material.

Plywood is made from thin sheets of wood veneer which are peeled from large logs and stacked together with the direction of each sheet's grain differing from the sheet next to it by 90 degrees. The sheets are then bonded under heat and pressure with strong adhesives. Waferwood, by comparison, was produced not from sheets of wood, but from compressed wafers, about the size of small potato chips. The chief advantage of waferwood was that it was derived from trees that previously had no market—trees such as aspen, alder, and other "soft" hardwoods. These were much more plentiful, faster growing, smaller in diameter, and much less expensive to grow and harvest than the trees from which plywood was produced.

I studied the waferwood samples being exhibited at the booth, asked some questions of the representatives from the Canadian company that was producing them and continued on through the exhibition hall. But no matter how hard I tried, I couldn't keep my mind off waferwood. I knew where the timber industry was, and I knew where it needed to be in the future. I also knew that in the coming years we needed to manufacture a product that did not rely on timber that was likely to be restricted from harvest, and wondered to myself if waferwood could be that product. We wouldn't have to own an acre of timberland to produce waferwood. We could buy it from farmers and ranchers who happened to own woodlots. The process of manufacturing waferwood was also easier and less costly than manufacturing plywood, meaning the price to consumers would be lower, as well. I returned a second and a third time to the booth to ask more questions. Never one to let moss grow under my feet, Jim Eisses and I were aboard the L-P jet that afternoon, on our way to Canada to tour three waferwood mills.

While I liked what I saw during those tours, I also identified some improvements that needed to be made in the product. For instance, I concluded that if waferwood panels were to be profitable, we could not just make one 4x8 panel at a time, as was the practice in the Canadian mills. My experience and intuition told me that 8x16 or 8x24 panels would be more economical, and could then be cut into four or six 4x8 panels. I also believed that waferwood needed to be sturdier. Plywood's strength comes from a process called "orientation," where several sheets of veneer are layered together, with the direction of the grain of the wood alternating between the different layers. I envisioned a similar process was necessary for waferwood, and knew just the person who could help—Dieter Simplekamp in Germany. Dieter and his company had made many large wood product presses for LP over the years, and I had always been impressed by his ingenuity and attention to detail.

I quickly phoned Dieter, told him about waferwood and asked if he could design and manufacture an orientation system and a press. Dieter assured me he could, and I immediately flew to Germany for more meetings and consultation. Somewhere over the Atlantic, Jim Eisses and I sketched out the machinery I thought was necessary for the task to strengthen small wafers of wood into a strong oriented panel, and then to cut that wood into four or six smaller 4x8 panels. I couldn't help but smile when the device we drew had a lot of serrated wheels for the wafers to go through, and looked a lot like Mama's ravioli cutter! Dieter approved of our concept, delivered the machinery on time, and L-P soon opened the first waferwood facility in Hayward, Wisconsin.

There were many in the industry who thought I was crazy for rushing so quickly into production of waferwood, predicting that it would never acquire a foothold in the market. Some timber executives publicly questioned my decision, pledging that their companies would never turn their backs on plywood. Our first waferwood plant, completed in 1978, was such a success that we immediately built a second one in Maine. We named our product "oriented strand board" (OSB for short) and by the time I left L-P in 1994, we had 17 OSB facilities up and running and three more under construction, with a combined production potential of over 6 billion board feet annually. Industry-wide, the acceptance of OSB has been phenomenal. By 2004, OSB—which some had once called "Merlo's folly"—had replaced much of the plywood market, accounting for 65% of residential floors utilizing panels, 75% of roofs and 85% of walls. In 2007, industry experts projected that North American oriented strand board production would reach 26.9 billion board feet from zero when we started.

Would OSB have gained such acceptance and popularity had I not happened to walk by that booth? It might have taken a few more years, but I like to think that someone else would have seen its potential. But would Louisiana-Pacific have been able to survive those few years, given that the government was putting a stranglehold on our timber supply? I don't know the answer to that question, but I do know that much of L-P's growth and success came because we were always ready to embrace change.

"God is in the water"

This simple reminder to not despoil our surroundings, she warned us not to pee-pee in the water because God was there, Mama shared this with my brothers and me each time we went out fishing, it has remained in my heart since my childhood. As I walk through the vineyards of my winery or inspect timberlands on my ranches in Eastern Oregon and California, nothing makes me more content than knowing that actions I will take will leave the land better than I found it.

Certainly the biggest challenge and frustration I experienced during my years in the forest products industry was dealing with the misperception that we were only out to make a buck, and that we were perfectly happy to chop down any tree that got in our way. And with each passing year, it seemed like more and more Americans somehow believed that it was morally wrong to cut a tree, regardless of how many you planted in its place.

I found it ironic that those who favored a ban on all logging never volunteered to do without their wood house or the countless wood-based products such as toilet paper that they used in their everyday life. The fact is that trees are a renewable resource, and if there is any truth to global warming, then we all know the best solution is to plant trees.

Nothing gives me more contentment than leaving the land better than I found it.

Let me be clear in saying that some logging practices of the past were certainly not as far-sighted and environmentally friendly as those of today. But by the late 1960's, those who wanted to succeed in the forest products industry understood that "cutting and running" without taking care to replant so a new generation of trees could be harvested again was harmful both to the environment and the balance sheet of your company both in the present and in the future.

Under my leadership, Louisiana-Pacific devoted countless hours and countless millions of dollars to programs and research aimed at improving the environment. One of the first actions I took as CEO was to begin construction of a nursery that grew seedlings to be planted on land we logged. I also implemented a very innovative program called "Tree Enterprise." Through this program, L-P's professional foresters were made available to assist private landowners by visiting their property and advising them on sustainable and environmentally-friendly forest management techniques.

And long before it was fashionable to save energy, many of our plants were using the bark and waste wood from the trees we harvested as fuel for fire to heat the water to make the steam to run a turbine to make electricity. At our plant in Samoa, California, we made all the electricity for the pulp mill, the town, and sold $100,000 of electricity each month to the local utility. We used the bark and sawdust because I insisted that if we were cutting a tree, then no part of it would be wasted. This was a philosophy learned by watching Mama in the kitchen. People came from miles around to eat her dinners—not knowing that the ingredients included cuts of meat that other people wouldn't buy and that were left over at the butcher shop.

No matter what we did, however, we got precisely no credit. In fact, Congress eventually seized more than 25,000 acres of prime timberland to expand Redwood National Park. This action would eventually cost American taxpayers $775 million dollars after a decade long legal battle, federal courts would eventually order the government to reimburse L-P for the timber. The courts could not, however, order the government to find new jobs for the hundreds of employees laid off due to the fact that our mills were left without any timber.

I wish I could say that the situation has improved in recent years, and that the American people and Congress now understand that trees are a renewable resource and that our forests require active professional—and not political management—but I can't. Because we have severely restricted humans from harvesting trees, we have watched these past few years that Mother Nature will harvest them in a much more environmentally destructive method— wild fires. Despite the fact that it makes perfect economic and environmental sense to try to salvage the remains of the burned timber before it decays and becomes fuel for future fires, so-called "environmentalists" race to the courts to ask for injunctions preventing any salvage activity. It would be funny if it weren't so sad.

If there's any hope that common sense might prevail in the future, it is because of organizations like the World Forestry Center in Portland, Oregon. Founded in 1964, the mission of the center is to educate and inform people about the world's forests and trees, and their importance to all life, in order to promote a balanced and sustainable future. The Center includes a 20,000 square foot museum, two working forests and the World Forest Institute, which has become a special cause of mine. I am especially proud of the World Forest Institute Fellowship Program—which happens to be housed in Merlo Hall. The Institute brings young forest products professionals from around the world to Portland for six to 12 months of study, research, and networking. Professionals from over 20 countries have come to the Institute since its inception, and my interaction with these intelligent and dedicated forestry professionals gives me cause for optimism.

The truly important things in life don't tarnish

I can't help but think how much my father lost out on by focusing so much of his time and attention on finding a precious metal, rather than on enjoying time spent with what is truly precious in life—family and friends.

Mama kept things in perspective. She was never rich in monetary terms, but if wealth can be measured in terms of the love of children and the admiration of friends, then she was a millionaire many times over.

When I was lying in bed as a young boy, with six feet of snow piled up outside the house, and dependent upon a brick heated in the oven and wrapped in a towel to keep me warm during the night, I could not have envisioned the financial success I would eventually achieve. I would be less than honest if I didn't confess that I enjoy many of the assets that money can buy, but I have also never forgotten that cash can not replace character, compassion, courage, or common sense.

One individual who was astonished at my lack of interest in feathering my own nest was the legendary American businessman and industrialist, Dr. Armand Hammer. Dr. Hammer and I had become friends through our membership in the American Academy of Achievement, and in May 1979, he summoned me to the Los Angeles, California headquarters of Occidental Petroleum, the giant corporation he had led for decades as Chairman and CEO. Prior to the meeting, word reached me that Dr. Hammer was interested in a merger between Occidental and L-P.

Dr. Hammer, who was then 80 years old, spent the first few minutes of our meeting asking me questions about L-P and the forest products industry. I answered the questions, and then asked him to confirm the purpose of the meeting. He replied that he was impressed by the growth and financial strength of Louisiana-Pacific and he was interested in a merger L-P with Occidental. Under his proposal, he would serve as CEO of the newly merged corporation, and I would stay on his heir apparent. He assured me that if I agreed to his proposal, I would end up with a compensation package in the neighborhood of $30 million.

It was certainly an attractive offer for me, but I didn't think it was the right decision for my company. I had done my research, too, and for a variety of reasons, had concluded that L-P's products and employees would not be a good match with the corporate structure in place at Occidental. I told Dr. Hammer that if he wanted his offer to be considered, it had to be put in writing, so I could take it to our Board of Directors. I also told him that if the Board accepted his offer, then I would not be part of the new corporate structure.

Dr. Hammer was stunned by my answer. He said that without my participation he was not interested in a merger, and he couldn't understand why I would not support a proposal that would make me a very wealthy man. I'm sure he also wouldn't have understood that my definition of success was being part of a team—a team that worked together, that trusted one another, and that was united behind a common mission. We had that team at L-P. I wasn't certain we would have it at Occidental Petroleum.

A few years after my dealings with Dr. Hammer, I received another offer that, if accepted, would have changed the future of Louisiana-Pacific. Sometime shortly after the discussions that led to the creation of Clotilde Merlo Park, my friend Sir Jimmy Goldsmith told me he was impressed with L-P's balance sheet and our prospects for continued success, and he asked what I thought about him buying the publicly-held L-P and taking it private. Sir Jimmy made it clear that I would still run the company, and that the move would be incredibly financially rewarding to me. He also discussed his vision of L-P—a vision that included the immediate selling off of a few of our divisions.

While I trusted and admired Sir Jimmy, and could easily envision working with him, I also knew that I had no interest in a proposal that that included jettisoning thousands of the employees who had done so much and worked so hard to make L-P the success it was. L-P was blessed with natural resources—our trees. We were also blessed with the most technologically advanced material resources—our mills and machinery. But I had no doubt, however, that it was our human resources, that were our most valuable asset, and that made it so rewarding to go to work each morning. I told Jimmy that if he wanted to go forward with his proposal, then he would have to do it without me, as I couldn't be part of plan that would break up the L-P team. Jimmy quickly turned his attention to his countless other projects and investments, and I very contentedly went back to my team.

Courage and Common sense will carry the day

"Courage and common sense." If I heard those words from Mama once, I heard them one thousand times. Mama possessed both of these qualities in great quantity, and she was firm in her belief that with them, all challenges could be overcome. I'll leave it up to others to determine if I exemplified these qualities during my career, but I do know that when the pressure was on and the going was at its toughest, my goal was to translate Mama's words into action.

Perhaps one of the most difficult times of my career occurred in 1983, when Louisiana-Pacific was the subject of a very bitter strike by the Lumber Production and Industrial Workers Union. The LPIWU represented about 1,700 L-P employees at eighteen of our facilities in California, Oregon, and Washington. For years, multi-party collective bargaining negotiations in the western wood products industry were conducted with the "big seven" timber companies, which included L-P, G-P, International Paper, and Weyerhauser. Once an agreement was reached, then all companies would be bound by the new contract.

As the time neared for a new agreement to be reached, I made the decision that L-P would opt out of the "big seven," and negotiate with the LPIWU on our own. My decision was a matter of principle. I was bothered by the fact that the new contract would guarantee new industry employees the same salary level as employees who had many years of experience. I thought this was unfair and disrespectful to the members of the L-P team who had worked hard and proven their worth to our company. I proposed a contract that would pay new employees a slightly lower salary than we paid to our experienced employees. After successfully completing one year of employment, those new employees would then receive the same rate of pay as our experienced employees.

I hoped that the union leadership would understand that my proposal was supportive and respectful of their members. Unfortunately, they not only turned down my offer, they also refused to sit down with me, and they refused to present my offer to their membership for a vote. Instead, they called for a strike, vowing to "teach Merlo a lesson" for my refusal to fall in line with the contract. The situation quickly escalated, as bomb threats were made against a number of our facilities, gun shots were fired at a company helicopter,

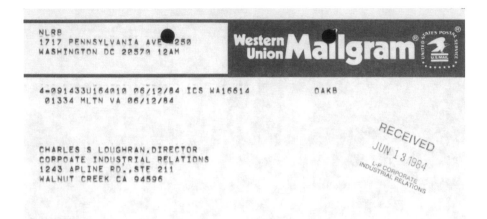

RE LOUISIANA PACIFIC CORP., CASE NOS. 19 CA 16243, 20 CA 18452
AND 32 CA 5996   THE EMPLOYER'S MOTION FOR RECONSIDERATION
IS SUSTAINED, THE DECISION SUSTAINING THE UNION'S APPEAL IS
REVOKED, AND THE APPEAL FROM THE REGIONAL DIRECTOR'S
REFUSAL TO ISSUE COMPLAINT IS DENIED. IN REACHING THIS
DECISION, FULL CONSIDERATION HAS BEEN GIVEN TO ALL EVIENCE
OBTAINED DURING THE INVESTIGATION, THE DOCUMENTS SUBMITTED
IN SUPPORT OF THE APPEAL, IN SUPPORT OF AND IN OPPOSITION TO
THE MOTION FOR RECONSIDERATION, AND THE ARGUMENTS
PRESENTED DURING THE UNION'S SEVERAL ORAL PRESENTATIONS.
DETAILED LETTER TO FOLLOW.

```
WILFORD W JOHANSEN,ACT GC
NLRB WSH DC

04960

17:25 EST

MGMCOMP
```

TO REPLY BY MAILGRAM MESSAGE, SEE REVERSE SIDE FOR WESTERN UNION'S TOLL - FREE PHONE NUMBERS anonymous death threats were made on me, and other unions joined the LPIWU in a public call for a boycott of L-P products. I guess they thought they could intimidate me into caving in to their demands. They guessed wrong.

Instead of intimidating me, their threats strengthened my resolve. I was secure in the courage of my convictions, and knew that the offer I had put on the table was the correct and responsible one for our employees, our stockholders, and the future of L-P. I vowed to keep our facilities open, and that is precisely what we did. Within three months, we were operating 15 of the 18 struck plants, thanks to a combination of nearly 500 union members who defied their leadership and crossed picket lines to return to work, and more than 675 permanent replacements. Better still, the rank and file union members understood what their leaders didn't—that the offer I had made for a new contract was a fair one. Since their leaders wouldn't allow them to vote on the offer, the members took the unusual step of demanding a vote to decertify the union, meaning that the union would no longer have the right to represent them. The first vote occurred at our sawmill in the central Oregon community of Prineville, and the vote was overwhelming to decertify. By mid-summer 1984, decertification elections had occurred at eighteen L-P facilities, and the union lost every one of them. The union leadership didn't give up. They went to the National Labor Relations Board to challenge the results of the elections, and they lost every challenge.

I had to give some of the union leaders credit for their persistence— and their creativity. At one of L-P's annual meetings, I looked out an audience that included a large number of people who I was told were all from a local church, and who were there for the specific purpose of heckling me during the question and answer session that followed our business session. As that hour long session neared its end, I began to wonder about how I would respond to the heckling when, much to my surprise, the church group rose as one and filed out. Those seated near by could hear the local union leader frantically tell them they were not supposed to be leaving. They also heard the church pastor reply, "You only paid us for an hour, and your hour is up."

There were some in the media who accused me of being a "union-buster." That was certainly not my hope or intention. My job as CEO was to do what I believed was best for all L-P employees and stockholders. From my point of view, the union leaders made two fundamental mistakes: They lacked the common sense to understand that it was better for prospective union members to be paid a slightly lower salary for their first six months than for all their members to not be employed at all. And they didn't think that L-P management had enough courage to resist their tactics of intimidation.

⁂

CHAPTER 10

Bossing Myself

THE MOST DIFFICULT DAYS of my 22 years as Chief Executive Officer of Louisiana-Pacific occurred over a several week span in the summer of 1995. Ironically, the year began on a high note, as the final 1994 sales and earnings figures were company records—$3.2 billion in sales, and $346 million in net after-tax earnings. Additionally, we had $315 million in the bank and had not a penny of debt. When I saw these numbers, I reflected with pride that just twenty years earlier, L-P's net sales were $386 million and earnings were $16 million. For the second time, The Wall Street Transcript named me the top CEO in the forest products industry, and I accepted the honor on behalf of our 13,000 employees working at 120 manufacturing facilities in 27 states.

While there were a number of legal and environmental challenges facing the company, I was confident that L-P's best days were still ahead, and that we would handle these challenges as we had throughout our history—by pulling together and working as a family. Indeed during my years as CEO, I prided myself in the fact that all decisions made by our board were made by a unanimous vote.

As the year went by, however, it became clear that our board of directors did not share my confidence in L-P's future. Policies and decisions they had once endorsed unanimously and that had not turned out exactly at we had hoped, were now regarded as my fault, and my fault alone. As someone who had long valued loyalty, I was disappointed with their behavior and their need to make me their fall guy, but I also understood that leadership carries a price, and sometimes the price is high. On July 31, 1995, L-P and I parted company.

While the sun came up the next morning—and has all the mornings since—it took me a while to get used to the fact that I would not be leaving my house and driving to my office or flying to one of our facilities. There were moments, of course, when I was angry—angry with colleagues who had turned their backs on me, and angry with myself, for not being able to convince them that L-P's future was as bright as I knew it was.

But as the weeks went on, I reflected that however difficult leaving L-P had been, Mama had weathered a countless number of days that were infinitely more challenging and stiflingly depressing. However, through her belief in God and her courage and common sense, she persevered through the death of her first husband, a journey with a young son to a new country, the abusive behavior of her second husband, and years and years of numbing poverty. She survived all this because she didn't look back and focus on what she might have lost. Rather, she focused on what she had. And that's just what I did. I was blessed with family and friends I loved very much, robust health, and financial resources. I reflected that I had spent my whole professional life answering to someone else—a boss or a board of directors. Perhaps it was now time to answer just to Harry Merlo. While one very satisfying chapter of my life had come to an end, it was now time to embark on a new and rewarding chapter.

Nearly twelve years have now passed since that new chapter began, and I can honestly say that it has been the most enjoyable time of my life. I have planted, logged, and replanted my own timber; subdivided and developed my own land; worked with my son, Harry, Jr., to develop the most beautiful vineyard lands in Sonoma County, California (and enjoyed the products from those vineyards); invested in my own venture funds, supported worthy causes through the Merlo Foundation, traveled the world on my own planes, entertained family and friends on my Alaska-based yacht. In short, I have been my own boss, and I look forward to bossing myself around for many more years to come.

When I reflect on my years at the helm of Louisiana-Pacific, the memories are all ones that bring a smile to my face. Above all, I remember my fellow L-P employees and the pride we felt in being members of the same team. Together, we built something great.

Since leaving L-P, I have still felt some loyalty to the company I led for so long, and have wished L-P nothing but the best. I confess that I was disappointed when the new management team moved the corporate headquarters from Portland, Oregon to Nashville, Tennessee. Additionally, while I am proud of the role I played in making L-P the leader in the oriented strand board market, I never put all our eggs in one basket and ensured that we offered a wide variety of products. L-P is now solely an OSB manufacturer, and along with the loss of product diversity, it also has lost roughly half the employees and half the revenue as it had during my last year as CEO.

As I look back on all the chapters of my life, I know in my heart that there is much in which I can take pride. But I also know that I have achieved nothing on my own. Rather, all I have achieved was accomplished only because of those who guided and mentored and supported the kid who was born and raised in a lumberyard: Mama; my brothers, Amiel, Pete, John and Frank; my sister, Caroline; Mr.

Musselman; Ralph Rounds; Mr. Pamplin; the dedicated employees of Louisiana-Pacific and Georgia-Pacific, including Flo Newton, Twila Bennett, Jai Cho, Ronnie Paul, Jim Eisses, John Hart, and the late Pam Selis, the public relations whiz who was the first female L-P employee to be named our "Man of the Year:" I also can't forget the crew who now work beside me at Merlo Corporation and Lago di Merlo Vineyards—a crew that includes Gary Maffei, who has been with me since my days at Georgia-Pacific, and who now runs the Merlo Foundation; my spiritual advisor and friend, the indomitable Father Chet Prusynski from the Universitiy of Portland; and, of course, my son, Harry, Jr., his wife, Billie, and my grandchildren Dominic and Anthony: To all, I say "grazie." A man could not ask for better loved ones, examples, mentors, and friends. And speaking of friends….

11

A Toast to Friendship

As a young boy, I could never have imagined that I would have the opportunity to cross paths and become acquainted with Presidents of the United States, Hollywood celebrities, and some of the most fascinating personalities of our time. Business success and my involvement in philanthropy, however, have allowed me to do just that. What follows are some glimpses of the individuals who, through their integrity and generosity, have impressed me the most:

Ronald Reagan: I first became acquainted with Ronald Reagan when he was Governor of California, and was a frequent speaker or guest at gatherings of California business leaders. I was not alone in recognizing his tremendous charisma and eloquence, and in urging him to set his sights to the White House. In the final days of his successful 1980 Presidential effort, I helped to organize a campaign rally at the Portland Airport. Even though countless concerns must have been weighing on him, Reagan could not have been more at ease as we waited for the rally to begin, and we reminisced about our days in California. Once Reagan became President, I was proud to be a strong supporter of his efforts to turn around America's spirits and economy, and our "Yes We Can" campaign often urged support for the President's policies. I became better acquainted with Reagan after he left the White House, when I made the Louisiana-Pacific jet available to him on several occasions for charitable events. I joined him on several of these flights, and was always struck by his unfailing graciousness.

One of my most treasured possessions the letter that President Reagan sent to be read at the dedication of Clotilde Merlo Park on August 29, 1987. The letter read as follows:

> *I am delighted to send warm greetings and congratulations to everyone gathered at Stirling City to dedicate the Clotilde Merlo Historical Park. This park now converts to public use a setting of natural beauty and historical value.*
>
> *Such an impressively conceived project pays eloquent tribute to the foresight and dedication of all those who have seen the possibilities, who rolled up their sleeves and went to work to make this land a source of enjoyment and learning for all.*
>
> *Of course, special recognition is due Harry Merlo, who has given much to his hometown through this park named for his mother. Caring for the places of an earlier time in our lives says much about our love of community and how we cherish our history and traditions.*
>
> *Thanks to Mr. Merlo and all of you, future generations will enjoy this park and find much food for thought in it. That's something you can be very proud of.*
>
> *Nancy joins me in congratulating you on your achievement and we send you our very best wishes. God bless you.*
>
> *Ronald Reagan*
> *President of the United States*

✯✯✯✯

RONALD REAGAN

June 25, 1992

Dear Harry:

I am writing to thank you for your kindness in providing your airplane to the United States Junior Chamber of Commerce for their Annual Convention in Portland, Oregon. I was pleased to have the opportunity to speak to that outstanding young group and I am grateful to you for your generosity in making it possible.

The flight and the crew were very enjoyable. My staff and I were touched by the additional care which was put into making our flight a pleasant one.

Your kind expression of friendship is certainly appreciated. Nancy joins me in sending our warmest best wishes.

Sincerely,

Ronald Reagan

Mr. Harry Merlo
Chairman
Louisiana-Pacific Corporation
111 S.W. 5th Avenue
Portland, Oregon 97204

Ronald Reagan and Harry Jr.

Gerald Ford: President Ford and I became acquainted through our mutual friendship with Edith Green, who represented Oregon in Congress for nearly two decades. Edith returned to Oregon following her retirement from Congress in 1975, and dedicated herself to worthy causes, including the construction of a home for troubled children. As Chairman of the Board of the Portland Salvation Army, I supported Edith's efforts and we worked together to raise funds for the construction of the home—which would eventually be named the "Green House," in Edith's honor. Ford came to Portland after his retirement from politics to help raise money for the Green House, and we would later socialize on several occasions in Palm Springs, California. Politicians are notorious for their egos, but President Ford appeared not to have one. He was humble, down-to-earth, and had a ready smile and a hearty laugh. People just don't get any more decent than Jerry Ford. He was a true national hero and was richly deserving of the tributes and praise that followed his passing in December 2006.

Colin Powell: If I could wave a magic wand and make Colin Powell our next President of the United States, I would do it. Colin and I became acquainted through our connection with two outstanding organizations, the Horatio Alger Association and the American Academy of Achievement.

The mission of the Horatio Alger Association is to honor the achievements of individuals who have succeeded in spite of adversity and to encourage young people to pursue their dreams through higher education. Last year, the Association awarded more than $12 million in scholarships to outstanding young people who have faced challenges and realize that a college education is the key to a better future. Similarly, the American Academy of Achievement brought outstanding students across America and around the world into direct personal contact with those who had found success in business, public service, arts and sciences, and other careers.

Born in the South Bronx to Jamaican immigrant parents, Powell found his life's calling when he joined the Reserve Officer Training Corps while attending City College in New York. He would go on, of course, to a distinguished career in the military and in public service, with stints as Chairman of the Joint Chiefs of Staff, National Security Advisor to President Reagan, and Secretary of State to President George W. Bush. The qualities of common sense and courage, which Mama emphasized throughout her life, can be found in great measure in Colin Powell.

Gerald Ford, Flo Newton, and Betty Ford

Colin Powell

Luciano Pavarotti and Flo Newton

Julio Gallo, left Ernest Gallo and Ted Balestreri

Tom Selleck

Dr. Maya Angelou

Flo Newton, Jack and Elaine LaLanne

I have been blessed with many wonderful friends, including from L-R, Red Emmerson, Flo Newton and timber executive Dan Dutton

Ray Park

During my service as Chair of the American Academy of Achievement, I presided over their annual gathering in San Francisco. I thought it would make for an unforgettable evening if we could have one of our association events aboard the aircraft carrier, the USS Carl Vinson, which was docked in the San Francisco harbor. I was told at several steps along the way that there was no way such a request would ever get approved, but one call to Colin Powell succeeded in cutting all the red tape.

Luciano Pavarotti: Just as my dad crossed paths with Caruso—the most famous opera singer of his time—on his journey to America, I was fortunate to cross paths with Pavarotti, the greatest opera singer of our time. As a supporter and patron of the Portland Opera, I provided financial backing to bring Pavarotti to Portland for two performances, and I sent the Louisiana-Pacific plane to pick him up in New York City. Pavarotti was impressed with our service and hospitality—perhaps a bit too impressed. When he arrived at my home that evening for a dinner reception he thanked me profusely for providing his transportation. "But Harry," he said, "You didn't have to put LP—my initials—on the tail of the airplane that picked me up." That night at a dinner at my house in his honor I sat him next to Dr. Albert Starr a world renowned heart specialist. In the course of the evening, I asked Luciano if he would like to see open heart surgery. He said, "yes, yes". The next day at St. Vincent's we could not find a gown big enough for him—the solution was to slice a short opening in the center of a

The Albert Starr academic center for cardiac surgery, 1/24/95

"Harry Merlo. A visionary in his own profession and a 'champion' of the arts and medical sciences."
- Albert Starr

bed sheet and out it over his head! He enjoyed himself so much that when he went home he went on a diet and lost 80 pounds. Then he got worried about what the weight loss was doing to the quality of his voice so he gave up the diet.

A few years later, we brought him back to Portland for another Opera—at this dinner in this honor I sat him next to Pete and Nancy Conrad—Commander of Apollo 12 who walked on the moon—Luciano could not get over the fact that we was sitting next to a man that had walked on the moon! Pavarotti's death in September of 2007 deprived the world of one of his most unforgettable voices.

Malcolm Forbes: Winston Churchill once said that meeting Franklin Roosevelt was like "opening a bottle of champagne." The same could be said about Malcolm Forbes. As the long-time publisher of *Forbes* magazine, which was required reading for every CEO in America, Malcolm was one of the most influential voices on economic and financial matters. But it was the world beyond Wall Street that most interested Malcolm. His passions included art collecting, hot air ballooning, riding Harley Davidson motorcycles, flying aboard his jet—named "The Capitalist Tool"—and hosting parties on his yacht, "Highlander." I was fortunate enough to be invited aboard the "Highlander" on several occasions, and my fellow passengers invariably included a mix of business titans, celebrities, and past and present members of Presidential cabinets. Malcolm was the consummate host, ensuring that the food and drink were fabulous, and presiding over a never ending game of gin rummy. I would often shake my head in wonder that Harry Merlo of Stirling City, California found himself in such opulent surroundings. From time to time, I still get a tear in my eye when I visit my beautiful wine cellar and see the last remaining bottle of 1907 Margaux that Malcolm gave to me from his New York library.

Archie "Red" Emmerson and Ray Park: The issue of *Forbes Magazine* that is annually read more than any other is the issue listing the "Forbes 400"—the richest 400 people in America. Two of the individuals on the list every year are "Red" Emmerson and Ray Park. Red and Ray are also two of my closest friends, and they would be so if they didn't have a penny to their names.

Red began his career by operating a small lumber mill with his father in the 1940's, and now, as the owner of over 2,000,000 acres of timberland, he trails only CNN founder Ted Turner in terms of ownership of private lands in the United States. His forest products company, Sierra Pacific Industries, is devoted to maintaining healthy forests and providing quality wood products to consumers, and it continues to thrive in a very tough business environment.

Ray also began his professional career in the lumber business, but eventually diversified into an impressive array of real estate, copper mining, and manufacturing. In addition, he once was a co-owner of Major League Baseball's Cleveland Indians.

Interestingly, neither Red nor Ray graduated from college, proving that business acumen is not bestowed on someone by a diploma. Rather, it is often better learned through hard work, common sense, experience, and an absolute assurance that their word is their bond. During my years at L-P, I had my eye on a Georgia-Pacific plywood plant in Logansport, Louisiana. I knew that if the word got out that Harry Merlo was interested in buying the plant, the price would skyrocket. Ray and I talked and he agreed to make a bid for the facility, with the assurance that L-P would then buy it from him. He soon struck a deal with G-P for a purchase price of $4.2 million. A few days later, a huge International Paper plywood facility just 30 miles away burnt to the ground. In desperate need of a plan to process their timber, IP called G-P and offered them $25 million for the Logansport plant. When IP learned that it had just been sold, they offered $20 million to Ray. When I learned what had occurred, I called Ray and told him that he was free to sell to International Paper. He refused, turning his back on a quick and easy $15.8 million profit for the simple reason that he had given me his word.

While they may be on a list of America's richest people, the best thing about Ray and Red is that could also be on a list of the most honest, entertaining, and down-to-earth people, as well.

Ernest and Julio Gallo: Given that my last name is Merlo, perhaps it was destiny that wine would play an important role in my life. As a young boy, I stomped grapes for my father's wine. Now, I have the pleasure of watching my grandchildren run through the vineyards of the winery my son and I operate. My involvement in the wine business has led to many lasting and wonderful friendships—none more memorable than my friendship with Ernest and Julio Gallo.

Ernest, who passed away in March, 2006 at the age of 97, and his brother, Julio, who passed away in 1993, were, like me, the sons of Italian immigrant parents who had immigrated to California. There were other similarities between our lives: Our fathers were both originally named "Giuseppe" and were called "Joe," once they arrived in America, and our mothers both operated a boardinghouse to help make ends meet for their family.

Through hard work, tireless and persuasive salesmanship, and a commitment to affordability, the Gallo brothers built a winery they began with $6,000 and three employees to a world famous business boasting more than 4,600 employees with products sold in more than 90 countries.

Whenever I sat down with the Gallo brothers—a meeting that usually included a glass or two of their product—I loved to hear stories about their early days in the business. Once, after I told Ernest about my plans for Lago di Merlo, he asked me how much our wine would cost. I said I don't know, but my son said if we don't charge enough they will think it's no good. It was then he shared a story I will always remember. During the prohibition era, Ernest could only sell wine to churches and synagogues, who used it for sacramental purposes. He said, Harry, I learned that lesson in 1937—Julio and I had a bill for $450 due in 4 months and we had no money. So, I went to NY to sell some wine and I stopped to see a Rabbi, and poured him a sample of the wine I had brought with me. The Rabbi smelled the wine, swirled it in his glass, took several sips, and finally asked what it cost. "It's 30 cents a gallon," Ernest replied.

The Rabbi waved his hand dismissively, exclaiming, "I don't want any of that cheap stuff."

Ernest thought for a moment and then asked, "Can you pay one dollar a gallon?"

"I can if I like it," the Rabbi declared.

Ernest, who had only brought one variety of wine with him, turned around, poured a glass from a different bottle of the exact same wine and handed it to the Rabbi. The Rabbi took several thoughtful sips and when he asked Ernest how much it cost he simply replied, "$1 a gallon"—the Rabbi joyfully exclaimed, "I'll take 450 gallons!

Tom Selleck: I didn't know Tom Selleck when he was honored by the American Academy of Achievement, but I felt like I did. Like most Americans, I had come to think that Selleck was a great deal like "Thomas Magnum, the character he portrayed on the long-running television series, "Magum, P.I." The fictional Thomas Magnum was funny, smart, humble, and always in search for ways to help people. You know what? It didn't take me long to realize that the real-life Tom Selleck possessed those same qualities. Selleck has put his fame to good use through extensive involvement in philanthropies and worthy causes. Selleck was inducted into the American Academy of Achievement at our event in San Francisco, which besides the evening aboard the U.S.S. Carl Vinson previously mentioned, also included a special black-tie dinner in the famed Alcatraz Prison. Several years later, in 2002, Tom surprised me by traveling to Portland to present me with the "Heart of Gold" award at a charity dinner. His first line when he took the microphone? "I became friends with Harry in Alcatraz."

Maya Angelou: Again, it was the Alger Association that allowed me to become friends with the inspiring author, poet and true national treasure. Maya and I shared many conversations about our childhood experiences, and about what she so eloquently terms the "loneliness of being poor and the frustration of not knowing where the future will lead." Whenever Maya speaks you can hear a pin drop, as everyone pauses to hear her unmistakable voice. One of the most memorable and humbling nights of my life was the October evening in 1993 when the National Multiple Sclerosis Foundation honored me with their Hope Award. A banquet room full of family, friends, and business colleagues gathered at the Portland Hilton for the annual awards dinner. Maya managed to steal the show—and she wasn't even there. The sponsors of the banquet had put together a video of several of my friends who could not be there for the evening, but who wanted to extend their best wishes. Leading off the video was Maya, who spoke a few words of greeting and then broke into song: "Look where we've all come from," she sang. "Look where we've all come from. Been brought out of the darkness and we're walking in the light. Look where we've all come from" There's no one I would rather hear sing—and there's no one who continues to inspire me to support organizations that provide food, shelter, and hope to those most in need—than Maya Angelou.

Dr. Robert Schuller and Arvella Schuller: Known worldwide for his weekly broadcast, "The Hour of Power," which is broadcast from the Crystal Cathedral in Garden Grove, California, Dr. Schuller is one of the most positive and inspiring individuals I ever had the privilege to meet. Although I was born, raised, and remain a Catholic, I admire those from any religion who encourage others to achieve great things through God. His famous admonition that "Tough times never last, but tough people do" is one that perfectly describes Mama's attitude. Dr. Schuller and I first crossed paths through the Academy of Achievement, and we hit it off from the start. I had the distinct honor of serving at the board of Dr. Schuller's ministries for ten years, where I also became friends with his wonderfully gracious wife, Arvella.

When I received the Hope Award, Dr. Schuller traveled to Portland to speak at the dinner ceremony. He inspired everyone there that evening with words, sharing an unforgettable story of a young Korean orphan who was raised in an orphanage sponsored by an American church. Eventually, the young boy was adopted by an American family, and grew to be a successful businessman, serving on the board of his local church. When he learned that the church was deeply in debt to a local bank, he paid off the entire indebtedness. "Anyone can count the seeds in an apple, but only God can count the apples in a seed," said Dr. Schuller, reminding us all that you never know how much good you give with one action.

Jack and Elaine LaLanne: My interest in physical fitness led to my friendship with this remarkable dynamo. Jack first gained fame in the 1950's when his television show allowed he and his dynamic wife, Elaine, to spread the gospel of exercise and eating right to millions of Americans. I was with Jack in Japan in 1979 as he celebrated his 65th in birthday in unique style—jumping, handcuffed and shackled, into the waters of Lake Ashinoko near Tokyo and towing 65 boats filled with 6,500 pounds of Louisiana-Pacific wood pulp. And I was with Jack five years later when he celebrated his 70th birthday in Long Beach, California, as he waded into the harbor for another amazing swim—handcuffed and shackled and fighting strong winds and currents, he towed 70 boats with 70 people for one mile to the bow of the Queen Mary. I plan on sticking around for his 100th birthday in 2014 just to see what he has up his sleeve.

Ion Tiriac: When I first met Ion in the mid-1980's, the man nicknamed "the mad Romanian" was famous in international tennis circles as the championship doubles partner of tennis legen Ilie Nastase and the coach of the great Boris Becker. Tiriac was familiar to tennis spectators and television viewers for his unique appearance—a haircut that sprouted in every direction and an impressive Fu Manchu moustache. Ion was unpredictable and a lot of fun, but I saw another side of him in the weeks and months following the collapse of Romania's communist government in late 1989 and early 1990. Within weeks of the overthrow of brutal dictator Nicolae Ceausescu, Tiriac came to me to me with a surprising request. Like others in his country, he was overjoyed with the demise of communism, and he desperately wanted democracy and private enterprise to succeed in his homeland. He knew Romania had aspen trees, and he thought that locating an OSB plan there might be a successful venture.

I agreed to fly to Romania to survey the situation. First, however, I asked the Portland-based humanitarian organization Northwest Medical Teams (now Medical Teams International) what medical supplies were most needed in Romania, and I filled my jet with those supplies. Ion and two large trucks greeted us upon arrival at the Romanian airport, and immediately transported the supplies to the orphanages that were operating in what can only be described as the most primitive of conditions. Tiriac then accompanied me to a helicopter where we flew to an incredibly elaborate palace that had once served as a vacation home for the communist leaders. The contrast between the opulence of the palace and the utter filthiness of the hospital was staggering and an eloquent indictment of the failure of communism.

I was very hopeful that L-P might be able to make an investment in the emergent Romanian democracy, but it was not to be as the available timber was of the wrong species and on rugged terrain overlooking the Danube River that made harvesting economically and environmentally unsustainable.

Perhaps what most amazed me about my journey to Romania was seeing the almost immediate transformation of my friend Ion from a tennis coach to an entrepreneur. Having witnessed first-hand his energy and vision, it has not surprised me that Ion has gone on to become the richest man in Romania, with a business empire giving him a net worth exceeding one billion dollars.

⚘⚘⚘

CHAPTER 12

Bon Appetit: From Mama, with Love

THE FOLLOWING RECIPES were some of Mama's favorites. Originally, of course, she made them without the benefit of electricity, cooking over a wood burning stove. You should feel free to use your oven! It should go without saying, however, that they will all taste a little better if they are enjoyed with a nice glass of Lago di Merlo wine!

Pomodori Con Basilico (Tomatoes with Basil)

6 ripe tomoatoes

salt to taste

1 cup fresh basil leaves, closely packed

1 clove garlic

⅓ cup olive oil

¾ cup pine nuts

½ cup Parmesan cheese, freshly grated

Preheat oven to 375 degrees F. Peel and core tomatoes. Squeeze tomatoes gently to remove seeds and turn them upside-down on layer of salt to drain.

Combine remaining ingredients in blender until pureed. (Mama did this with a mortar and pestle.)

Salt tomatoes inside and out and fill with equal portions of basil mixture. Bake in oven for approximately 30 minutes. Chill and serve cold. Serves 6 as an appetizer.

Zuccine Ripieni (Stuffed Zucchini)
1 cup ground ham
½ cup soft breadcrumbs
½ teaspoon mustard
½ teaspoon each salt and pepper
2 tablespoons minced onion
½ cup tomato sauce
½ cup grated Parmesan cheese
2 pounds zucchini
¼ cup olive oil
1 clove garlic, chopped
1 ½ teaspoons cornstarch

Preheat overn to 350 degrees F. In mixing bowl, combine ham, breadcrums, mustard, salt, pepper, onion and Parmesan.

Cook zucchini for 5 minutes in salted water. Wash zucchini and cut into halves lengthwise. Scoop out centers and stuff with ham mixture. Slice cross sections of zucchini into desired portions.

Place zucchini in baking pan, drizzle with olive oil and sprinkle with chopped garlic. Cover and bake for 45 to 50 minutes until tender. Remove from pan, saving juices.

Mix cornstarch with tomato sauce and stir into pan. Cook over low heat until thickened. Skim off excess fat, spoon tomato sauce over zucchini.

Serves 6

Pasta di Raviolo (Ravioli dough)

12 Cups flour

5 eggs

2 tablespoons olive oil

3 ½ cups lukewarm water

Sift flour onto large workspace. Make a "well" in the center. Add eggs and olive oil. Knead with hands until partially mixed. Add lukewarm water, a little at a time, and continue mixing. Work dough through pasta machine several times.

(Mama had no modern conveniences such as a pasta machine and had to roll the dough with a large, long rolling pin until she reached the desired thickness. Your job can be made easier with the use of a pasta machine, or you can choose to roll the dough out on a board just the way Mama did.)

Ripieno di Carne E Sugo Per Ravioli (Meat filling and sauce for ravioli)

4 pound pork roast

5 pound beef roast

10 sprigs rosemary

10 cloves garlic

1 tablespoon nutmeg

salt and pepper to taste

3 tablespoons olive oil

4 onions

4 carrots

5 celery stalks

2 cups red wine

2 bunches spinach

2 tbs. melted butter

2 or 3 slices of bread soaked in hot milk

¼ cup parlsey, chopped

3 gloves garlic, chopped

1 teaspoon marjoram

1 cup Parmesan cheese, grated

8 eggs

Preheat oven to 400 degrees F. Insert 5 sprigs of rosemary and 5 cloves(whole) of garlic into park roast and insert 5 sprigs of rosemary and 5 cloves (whole) of garlic into beef roast. Sprinkle roast with nutmeg, salt and pepper.

Warm 3 tablespoons olive oil in pan. Add roasts, onions, carrots, and celery stalks, all quartered into large pieces. Add more salt and pepper.

Put into oven and cook for 1 ½ hours. When meat is nearly done, pour wine over top.

Clean and cook spinach and let cool. Chop spinach and add 2 tablespoons melted butter.

Remove meat after 2 hours. Cut meat away from bones and cool. (save bones) Grind meat. Add spinach and work together.

Add 2 or 3 slices of bread soaked in hot milk. Add parsley, garlic and marjoram. Add Parmesan, a little at a time, mixing as you go. Add eggs, one at a time, continuing to mix. Add more salt, pepper, and nutmeg. (Add additional egg if mixture is too stiff.)

Fill raviolis with this mixture. Over thin dough, place 1 teaspoon of filling at 1-inch intervals. Fold dough over filling and cut with ravioli cutter. Seal and cook ravioli in boiling salted water until ravioli rises to surface.

SAUCE

Meat bones from ravioli filling recipe

2 cups dried porcini mushrooms, chopped

2 tablespoons flour

3 cans tomato paste and equal amount water

Two 15 ounce cans tomato sauce and equal amounts water

One 15 ounce can of reserved mushroom water

Soak porcini mushrooms in 15 ounces hot water and cover. Drain mushrooms and let cool (save water).

In original roast pan, add all ingredients. Return pan to oven, cook slowly and stir occasionally. After sauce begins to bubble, reduce heat to 300 degrees. Continue to cook for 2 ½ to 3 hours.

Skim fat from sauce. Strain. Add water as necessary for proper consistency. Cook again for flavor if necessary.

Pollo Con Salsa Verde (Chicken with Green Sauce)

1 frying chicken cut into pieces

2 tbs. butter

¼ cup olive oil

1 cup parsley, minced

2 cloves garlic, minced

2 tbs. flour

1 cup chicken stock

1 cup white wine

salt and pepper to taste

½ tsp. nutmeg

1 cup mushrooms, fresh or dried

Saute chicken with olive oil in skillet, sprinkle with salt, pepper, and nutmeg. Put chicken aside. In original skillet, add butter, parsley and garlic. Add mushrooms and sauté. Add chicken stock and wine. Stir constantly and add flour. Taste, re-season with salt and pepper if necessary.

Either bake in covered dish at 350 degrees for one hour or cover the skillet and simmer for one hour.

★★★

YEAR ENDED DECEMBER 31 (IN MILLIONS)	1994	1993	1992
Total sales — point of origin			
U.S.	$2,937	$2,482	$2,153
Canada and other	158	83	71
Intersegment sales to U.S.	(55)	(54)	(39)
Total sales	$3,040	$2,511	$2,185
Export sales (included above)	$ 371	$ 252	$ 339
Operating profit (loss)			
U.S.	$ 585	$ 479	$ 324
Canada and other	46	24	20
Total operating profit	$ 631	$ 503	$ 344
Identifiable assets			
U.S.	$2,325	$2,116	$1,911
Canada	363	341	295
All other	28	9	—
Total assets	$2,716	$2,466	$2,206

Information about L-P's industry segments is as follows:

YEAR ENDED DECEMBER 31 (IN MILLIONS)	1994	1993	1992
Total sales			
Building products	$2,831	$2,434	$2,013
Pulp	220	85	185
Intersegment sales to pulp	(11)	(8)	(13)
Total sales	$3,040	$2,511	$2,185
Operating profit (loss)			
Building products	$ 636	$ 562	$ 364
Pulp	(5)	(59)	(20)
Total operating profit	631	503	344
Unallocated expense, net	(72)	(70)	(47)
Interest, net	1	(5)	(14)
Income before taxes, minority interest and accounting changes	$ 560	$ 428	$ 283
Identifiable assets			
Building products	$1,146	$1,040	$ 934
Pulp	440	423	403
Timber, timberlands, logging equipment and roads	733	710	568
Unallocated assets	397	293	301
Total assets	$2,716	$2,466	$2,206
Depreciation, amortization and cost of timber harvested			
Building products	$ 162	$ 157	$ 137
Pulp	29	21	22
Capital expenditures			
Building products	228	144	90
Pulp	30	46	33
Timber, timberlands, logging equipment and roads	92	118	62

⅄⅄⅄⅄

Louisiana-Pacific Corporation and Subsidiaries
MANUFACTURING FACILITIES

PLANT CAPACITIES AT DECEMBER 31, 1994

SAWMILLS
(Board feet, 2 shifts, 5 days; *1 shift, 5 days)

	Metric 1) Capacities	Normal 2) Capacities
Redwood/Whitewood (3 plants)		
Big Lagoon, CA (E)	33	20*
Samoa, CA (E)	163	100
Ukiah, CA (E) (4th Qtr. 95 startup)	195	120
Other Western Lumber (9 plants)		
Annette, AK (A)	112	70
Chilco, ID (B)	122	75
Ketchikan, AK (A)	98	60
Pilot Rock, OR (B) (3 shifts)	122	75
Post Falls, ID (B)	41	25
Priest River, ID (B)	65	40*
Sandpoint, ID (remanufacturing) (B)	—	—
Sundre, Alberta, Canada (B)	106	65
Walla Walla, WA (B) (3 shifts)	163	100
Western Stud Mills (8 plants)		
Belgrade, MT (B)	148	90
Deer Lodge, MT (B) (3 shifts)	131	80
Fort Bragg, CA (also redwood) (E)	114	70
Libby, MT (B)	41	25*
Moyie Springs, ID (B)	148	90
Saratoga, WY (B)	148	90
Tacoma, WA (B)	98	60
Willits, CA (also redwood) (E)	90	55
Southern Lumber (27 plants)		
Bernice, LA (C)	81	50*
Bon Weir, TX (C)	41	25*
Braggs, AL (C)	41	25*
Carthage, TX (C)	98	60*
Cleveland, TX (2 plants) (C)	148	90*
Crestview, FL (C)	81	50*
Eatonton, GA (C)	65	40*
Evergreen, AL (C)	73	45*
Grenada, MS (C)	81	50*
Hattiesburg, MS (C)	81	50*
Hazelhurst, GA (C)	41	25*
Henderson, NC (C)	81	50*
Jasper, TX (2 plants) (C)	156	95*
Kountze, TX (C)	24	15*
Lockhart, AL (C)	50	30*
Marianna, FL (C)	57	35*
Nashville, NC (C)	41	25*
New Waverly, TX (C)	163	100*
Philadelphia, MS (C)	81	50*
Pittsboro, NC (C)	16	10*
Statesboro, GA (C)	41	25*
Trinity, TX (C)	33	20*
Waynesboro, GA (C)	98	60*
Westbay, FL (C)	81	50*
Winnfield, LA (C)	81	50*
Total Lumber Capacity (47 plants)	3,972	2,435

PANEL PRODUCTS PLANTS

Softwood Plywood Plants
(⅜-inch basis, square feet, 2 shifts, 5 days)

	Metric 1) Capacities	Normal 2) Capacities
Bon Weir, TX (C)	245	275
Cleveland, TX (C)	245	275
Jasper, TX (C)	132	150
Logansport, LA (C)	198	225
Lufkin, TX (C)	156	175
New Waverly, TX (C)	250	280
Urania, LA (C)	221	250
Total Softwood Plywood Capacity (7 plants)	1,447	1,630

Inner-Seal OSB Plants
(⅜-inch basis, square feet, 3 shifts, 7 days;* 2 shifts, 7 days)

	Metric 1) Capacities	Normal 2) Capacities
Chilco, ID (B)	133	150
Corrigan, TX (C)	120	135*
Dawson Creek, B.C. Canada (B)	355	400
Dungannon, VA (B)	124	140
Hanceville, AL (C)	284	320
Hayward, WI (2 plants) (B)	444	500
Houlton, ME (B)	231	260
Jackson County, GA (C)	284	320
Jasper, TX (C) (4th Qtr. 95 startup)	311	350
Montrose, CO (B)	129	145
Newberry, MI (B)	111	125
New Waverly, TX (C)	40	45*
Roxboro, NC (C) (4th Qtr. 95 startup)	311	350
Sagola, MI (B)	355	400
Silsbee, TX (C)	284	320
Swan River, Manitoba Canada (B) (4th Qtr. 95 startup)	444	500
Tomahawk, WI (B)	133	150
Two Harbors, MN (B)	120	135
Urania, LA (C)	102	115*
Waterford, Ireland (B) (4th Qtr. 95 startup)	355	400
Total OSB Capacity (21 plants)	4,670	5,260

Medium Density Fiberboard Plants
(¼-inch basis, square feet, 3 shifts, 7 days)

	Metric 1) Capacities	Normal 2) Capacities
Eufaula, AL (C)	221	125
Oroville, CA (E)	88	50
Urania, LA (C)	88	50
Total Medium Density Fiberboard Capacity (3 plants)	397	225

Particleboard Plants
(¾-inch basis, square feet, 3 shifts, 7 days)

	Metric 1) Capacities	Normal 2) Capacities
Arcata, CA (E)	221	125
Missoula, MT (B)	274	155
Silsbee, TX (C)	142	80
Total Particleboard Capacity (3 plants)	637	360

Hardboard Plant
(⅛-inch basis, square feet, 3 shifts, 7 days)

	Metric 1) Capacities	Normal 2) Capacities
Oroville, CA (E)	65	220

1) Metric capacities in thousand cubic meters
2) Normal capacities in millions of units unless otherwise noted

Louisiana-Pacific Corporation and Subsidiaries
MANUFACTURING FACILITIES

PLANT CAPACITIES AT DECEMBER 31, 1994

EXECUTIVE OFFICERS

Harry A. Merlo
Chairman and President

James Eisses[1]
Executive Vice President

Ronald L. Paul[2]
Vice President, Operations

ADMINISTRATION

Jai P. Cho
General Manager,
Export Sales

James F. Ellisor[1]
Controller, Operations and
Chief Accounting Officer

Harley C. Harrison
Director, Aviation

William L. Hebert
Treasurer and
Chief Financial Officer

Anton C. Kirchhof, Jr.
General Counsel and
Corporate Secretary

Barry Lacter
Public Relations
Manager

Gary R. Maffei
Director, Personnel
and Employee Benefits

Pamela A. Selis
Director, Corporate
Communications

Elizabeth T. Smith
Director,
Environmental Affairs

Dwayne Tofell[1]
Director, Taxes

[1]Located at the company's Northern
Division headquarters
[2]Located at the company's Southern
Division headquarters

HEADQUARTERS LOCATIONS

Corporate Offices
111 S.W. Fifth Avenue,
Portland, OR 97204
503/221-0800
503/796-0204 – FAX

Ketchikan Pulp Co.
Ralph D. Lewis,
President and
General Manager
P.O. Box 6600,
Ketchikan, AK 99901
907/225-2151
907/225-8260 – FAX

Northern Division
James Eisses,
Executive Vice President
P.O. Box 4000-98
Hayden Lake, ID 83835
208/772-6011
208/772-9636 – FAX

Southern Division
Ronald L. Paul,
Vice President, Operations
P.O. Box 3107,
Conroe, TX 77305
409/756-0541
409/760-5999 – FAX

Weather-Seal Division
Keith Matheney,
General Manager
324 Wooster Road North,
Barberton, OH 44203
216/745-1661
216/745-7492 – FAX

Western Division
Robert M. Simpson,
General Manager
P.O. Box 158,
Samoa, CA 95564
707/443-7511
707/443-0522 – FAX

Creative Point, Inc.
Jerry M. Long,
President
4121 Clipper Court
Fremont, CA 94538
510/659-8222
510/659-8260 – FAX

STOCKHOLDER INFORMATION

Annual Meeting
The annual meeting of stockholders will be held at 10:30 a.m., local time, Monday, May 1, 1995, at John Ascuaga's Nugget, 1100 Nugget Avenue, Sparks, Nevada. Louisiana-Pacific Corporation's Form 10-K Annual Report to the Securities and Exchange Commission will be available upon written request to the Director of Corporate Communications.

Dividend Reinvestment
Holders of the company's common stock may automatically reinvest dividends toward purchase of additional shares of the company's common stock. For a copy of a brochure describing the plan and an application, contact: First Chicago Trust Company of New York, Dividend Reinvestment Plans — Louisiana-Pacific, P.O. Box 2598, Jersey City, NJ 07303-2598. (201) 324-0498.

Ticker Symbol: LPX
Louisiana-Pacific Corporation's common stock is listed on the New York Stock Exchange.
Dow-Jones newspaper quotations symbol: LaPac.

Transfer Agent and Registrar:
First Chicago Trust Company of New York
Jersey City, New Jersey

Investor Relations Contact:
William L. Hebert

Shareholder Services:
Ann B. Mahone

Auditors:
Arthur Andersen LLP, Portland, Oregon

Counsel:
Miller, Nash, Wiener, Hager & Carlsen, Portland, Oregon.

About the Company:
Louisiana-Pacific Corporation, headquartered in Portland, Oregon, is a major manufacturer of building materials, industrial wood products and pulp. L-P is known for innovation in developing new, affordable, environmentally advanced products for homebuilders, remodelers, commercial builders, and furniture and cabinet manufacturers. Most of these new products are made from plentiful, noncontroversial resources — not old growth. Some of L-P's building products use recycled paper as a fiber source. The company is also known for its commitment to totally chlorine-free pulp.

We were formed in 1973 as a spin-off from Georgia-Pacific. Today, we have stewardship over two million acres of timberland and operate facilities in 27 U.S. states, Mexico, Ireland and Canada.

Louisiana-Pacific is an Equal Opportunity Employer.

L-P, Louisiana-Pacific, Inner-Seal, FiberBond, "Doing something about it" and Nature Guard are registered trademarks of Louisiana-Pacific Corporation. Totally Green is a trademark of Louisiana-Pacific Corporation.

American Academy of Achievement Salutes Harry Merlo, Grand Patron of the Academy and it's annual tribute to America's most inspiring giants of accomplishment. June 26, 1982.

For the Golden Plate Awards Council
Edward Asner, Olivia de Havilland, James A. Michener, James Stewart, Clint Eastwood, Alex Haley, Dr. Jonas Salk, Edward Teller, Dr. Michael E. DeBakey. Gen. David C. Jones, John J. Sirica, William H. Webster

Acknowledgements

TEAMWORK IS A KEY INGREDIENT to achieving success in sports, in business, and in life. I have also learned that it is necessary in the writing of a book. This book would not have been possible without the extensive researching and writing completed by Ron Arnold. Ron's work remained in my file for over a decade, until friends and colleagues again urged me to share my life's journey. Kerry Tymchuk then picked up the baton and helped make this book a reality, becoming a friend in the process. Other members of the team included John and Christina Blackwell, who provided perceptive suggestions and constant encouragement; Brian Parrott, who opened up his tennis scrapbooks and his memories; and Linda Hanson, my executive assistant, who keeps me moving forward, and who kept Vintage Merlo moving forward, as well. Finally, thanks to Brandy, my faithful canine companion, who sat patiently through many writing and editing sessions with nary a bark.